DRAMA CLA

The Drama Classics ser
plays in affordable pape.   ۔۔ ۔ مudents, actors
and theatregoers. The hallmarks of the series are accessible
introductions, uncluttered texts and an overall theatrical
perspective.

Given that readers may be encountering a particular play for
the first time, the introduction seeks to fill in the theatrical/
historical background and to outline the chief themes rather
than concentrate on interpretational and textual analysis.
Similarly the play-texts themselves are free of footnotes and
other interpolations: instead there is an end-glossary of
'difficult' words and phrases.

The texts of the English-language plays in the series
have been prepared taking full account of all existing
scholarship. The foreign-language plays have been newly
translated into a modern English that is both actable and
accurate: many of the translators regularly have their work
staged professionally.

Edited until his early death by Kenneth McLeish, the Drama
Classics series continues with his aim of providing a first-class
library of dramatic literature representing the best of world
theatre.

Associate editors:
Professor Trevor R. Griffiths
Professor in Humanities, University of Exeter
Dr Colin Counsell
Senior Lecturer in Theatre Studies and Performing Arts

DRAMA CLASSICS *the first hundred*

*The publishers welcome
suggestions for further titles*

DRAMA CLASSICS

THE RECRUITING OFFICER

by
George Farquhar

edited and introduced by
Simon Trussler

NICK HERN BOOKS
London
www.nickhernbooks.co.uk

A Drama Classic

This edition of *The Recruiting Officer* first published in Great Britain as a paperback original in 1997 by Nick Hern Books Ltd, The Glasshouse, 49a Goldhawk Road, London W12 8QP

Reprinted 2006, 2009, 2013

Copyright in the introduction © 1997 Nick Hern Books Ltd
Copyright in this edition of the text © 1997 Simon Trussler

Typeset by Country Setting, Kingsdown, Kent CT14 8ES
Printed by Mimeo Ltd, Huntingdon, Cambridgeshire PE29 6XX

A CIP catalogue record for this book is available from the British Library

ISBN 978 1 85459 340 5

Introduction

George Farquhar (*c*. 1677-1707)

George Farquhar was born in Londonderry in northern Ireland, probably in 1677, and would have been verging on adolescence when the recently deposed James II besieged that city in 1689. His father, as an Anglican clergyman, was a target for plunder and died soon afterwards, while the barely teenage George is said to have fought (on King William's victorious side) in the subsequent Battle of the Boyne in 1690 – which imposed the protestant succession (and a great deal of continuing grief) upon the Catholic majority in Ireland.

Prematurely experienced in both the sorrows and the heroisms of war, Farquhar proceeded from the local grammar school to Trinity College, Dublin, in 1694, then in quick succession fell in love with the theatre, performed at the Smock Alley playhouse in Dublin, gave up acting after accidentally killing a fellow-performer in a stage duel, and, like his lifelong friend and compatriot Robert Wilks, determined on a future in London. Here, Farquhar's first comedy, *Love and a Bottle*, was performed in 1698; but his precocious success as a playwright (discussed in more detail in the section 'The Comic Worlds of George Farquhar', on p. vii) was interrupted by the renewal of war with France in 1702. In 1704 he was granted a commission as a Lieutenant of Grenadiers and sent off on a recruiting campaign to the Midlands.

Meanwhile, in 1703, Farquhar had married – in expectations of an income from his wife's fortune, which proved to be non-existent. Indeed, he very soon found himself needing to provide for their two daughters as well – at a time when he was beginning to feel the effects of the wasting illness which is now thought to have been tuberculosis. He drew on his provincial experiences in both of his last two plays, *The Recruiting Officer* and *The Beaux Stratagem* (and arguably on his marriage in the latter), but his rapidly declining health prevented him from building on their success, and he died in poverty in late May 1707. His friend Wilks paid for his funeral.

The Recruiting Officer: **What Happens in the Play**

Captain Plume and his wily companion Sergeant Kite arrive on
a recruiting campaign in Shrewsbury, where the pair set out to cheat
or flatter the country folk into volunteering for the wars. Plume
renews his friendship with a local magistrate, Balance, and his lively
and beautiful daughter Silvia. Balance looks approvingly on the
young officer he once resembled – but fears for the virtue of his
daughter, who ill-conceals her love for the gallant Captain. Hopes
of a more honourable alliance are dashed when news arrives of the
death of Balance's only son, leaving Silvia an heiress wealthy beyond
Plume's aspirations.

Silvia's cousin Melinda has also come unexpectedly into an inheritance, making her a suitable match for Plume's friend Worthy. But
Melinda, despising her lover's earlier attempts to make her his kept
mistress, plays hard to get, encouraging the attentions of another
recruiting campaigner, the freewheeling Captain Brazen. Plume and
Brazen both set out to recruit the handsome Jack Wilful – in reality
Silvia, who prefers male disguise to the rustic retreat ordered by her
father. Despite Silvia's suspicions, Plume's attentions to the local
beauty Rose appear designed less to attract the girl into his bed than
her suitors and her brother into the army. Kite, disguised as a
fortune-teller, tricks more of the locals into joining up – and Melinda
into believing that Worthy will go to his death in the wars if she does
not secure him by the following morning.

After a disappointing night spent as 'Wilful's' bedfellow, Rose and
her supposed seducer are taken before the magistrates, where, along
with other petty offenders, the still disguised Silvia is ordered into
Plume's service by her own father – as she had planned. Although a
further complication leads Worthy to believe that Melinda is about
to elope with Brazen, the couple are eventually betrothed to their
mutual satisfaction – as also are Silvia and her Captain, following
revelations which satisfy Balance of Plume's honour. Now intending
to resign a martial for a marital role, Plume hands over to Brazen
the recruits he had raised, while Rose is taken into service as lady's
maid to Silvia.

The Comic Worlds of George Farquhar

The work of George Farquhar fits awkwardly into that over-extended category which critics have labelled 'Restoration comedy'. Charles II had been 'restored' (following his father's execution and the 'interregnum' under Cromwell) in 1660, and the honeymoon he had enjoyed with his subjects was well over by 1677, the probable year of Farquhar's birth. Shortly afterwards, the crisis caused by the probability that the Catholic James would succeed his brother to the throne set in motion the struggle for a constitutional monarchy – a struggle which led to King James's deposition during the 'bloodless revolution' of 1688-89, and the enthronement of William and Mary. The bourgeois sensibility of this royal couple proved well-suited to the changing national mood, as pursuit of the pleasure principle (so marked a feature of Charles II's reign) gave way before the sterner demands of the protestant work ethic.

It is true that Farquhar's near contemporaries Congreve and Vanbrugh (who both outlived him by some twenty years) continued to develop a dramatic tradition – of high-style, high-life 'comedy of manners', rooted in sexual dalliance – begun during the Restoration proper by Dryden, Etherege, Wycherley and Aphra Behn. But both Congreve and Vanbrugh gave up writing for the theatre soon after Jeremy Collier's influential anti-theatrical polemic, *A Short View of the Immorality and Profaneness of the English Stage*, published in 1698, had given voice to the changed moral climate of the times. Of the dramatists who have survived in the modern repertoire, Farquhar alone, it seems, found a spiritual as well as a chronological home in the society and the theatre of the years around the turn of the seventeenth and eighteenth centuries.

Even so, he was barely twenty when he wrote his first play, *Love and a Bottle*, and could not at first afford (or perhaps did not yet know how to manage) so new and personal a dramatic mode. Then in 1699, with *The Constant Couple*, he wrote a comedy in which conventional sexual pursuits were driven in part by new imperatives of cash and class – and the play found a responsive audience, proving the success of the season. But Farquhar evidently rested a little too long on the income and the laurels it brought him: and when, after eighteen months, he came up with a sequel, *Sir Harry Wildair*, the play suffered, as do so many sequels, from the law of diminishing returns – though it managed a respectable first run, presumably on the strength of its audience's curiosity to see how all the familiar characters would make out after marriage.

Farquhar's next play, *The Inconstant*, which took over and simplified the plot of John Fletcher's late Jacobean comedy *The Wild Goose Chase*, survived to its sixth night; but the death of King William in March 1702 cut short the theatrical season, and Farquhar set to work on *The Twin-Rivals*, which had its first night in December of the same year. The play is very tightly plotted around a younger brother's attempt to defraud his marginally older twin out of his inheritance. Sex here not only comes an acknowledged second to money but is rather more closely connected with childbirth than theatrical convention usually allowed. There is more dramatic interest in the fraudulent lordling's demonstration of his unworthiness than in his eventual exposure, and although the play has not quite caught the tone of voice in which to be 'seriously funny', it does strike out in the new direction which Farquhar was shortly to follow through in *The Recruiting Officer* and *The Beaux Stratagem*.

In between, the short farce *The Stage-Coach* – dealing with the 'mistakes of a night', as true love blossoms in the attempt to save a girl from her guardian's preferred suitor – also anticipated Farquhar's last two plays, in its country setting of an inn. As Eric Rothstein says, 'it makes one hungry for the work he did not do' between its production late in 1703 and 1706. On the other hand, it was no doubt precisely Farquhar's escape from the incestuous world of literary and theatrical London during these years that tempered his final plays with the hard edge of experience – his brief military career providing a background for *The Recruiting Officer* (1706), and his own unfortunate marriage perhaps a source for his portrayal of sexual incompatibility in *The Beaux Stratagem* (1707).

In these, the great plays of his maturity, Farquhar does not abandon 'mannered' comedy as such; instead he transplants it, choosing locations outside London and including characters of the middling-to-lower social orders. In the process, not only are old conventions and rivalries – between town and country, between leisured elegance and workaday greed – given quite a different focus, but the characters gain a capacity for experiencing subtler nuances of pleasure, and (perhaps more significantly) even for experiencing pain. The modern critic Robert Hume makes a useful distinction between the 'hard' comedy of Congreve and Vanbrugh, as late exponents of the Restoration mode, and the 'humane' school which (along with Collier's censure) soon provoked both writers into abandoning playwriting. In the work of Farquhar alone do we find the broader sympathies of the new mode combined with the wit and verve of the old.

Until well into the twentieth century, however, both *The Recruiting Officer* and *The Beaux Stratagem* tended to be viewed rather as Restoration comedies *manqués*. In revival rougher edges were apologetically honed, and creative tensions resolved rather than dramatically sustained. Ironically, it took a foreigner, Bertolt Brecht, to recognise the sterner stuff of which *The Recruiting Officer* was made, in his own updated version entitled *Drums and Trumpets:* and the English director Bill Gaskill acknowledged this Brechtian influence when, in his National Theatre production of 1964, he worked not to transplant fashionable metropolitan society into the provinces, but to relish and reveal the sharper local colours and broader social spectrum here captured by Farquhar. More recently, in a revival at the Royal Court Theatre in 1988, Max Stafford-Clark was able to assimilate such insights, while sustaining the comic irony in a production which seemed aptly postmodern in combining a laid-back temper and a brisk tempo – as also in its recognition of Farquhar's mixed feelings about the seedy business of recruiting.

In Farquhar's last play, *The Beaux Stratagem*, two handsome but impoverished gallants take it in turns to play master and servant in their search for an alliance to mend their fortunes. They capture the hearts not only of the desired heiress, but of her sister, a married woman – whose husband's eventual consent to divorce typifies the play's blending of comic convenience with sexual and economic realism. Such a mood also characterises *The Recruiting Officer*, where Farquhar skilfully modifies theatrical conventions and 'mannered' characters to portray the actualities of social life and the politico-economic pressures of the first decade of the eighteenth century.

Whig and Tory, Town and Country

Twice within a generation Farquhar's England had experienced a decisive political change which effected and reflected a social consensus against political extremes. With the Restoration of 1660 puritanism and republicanism had been repudiated: then, in 1689, with the deposition of James II in favour of William and Mary, the combination of Catholicism and authoritarianism for which Louis XIV of France provided a working model was no less decisively rejected. In retrospect, the 'constitutional' monarchy which resulted may seem part of a natural process of evolutionary change; at the time it was no less precarious than any other of the power structures of the seventeenth century.

Party groupings now emerged, reflecting the conflicting class interests involved in these changes. So-called 'Tories' were driven ideologically by a belief in the monarchy and the established church, and their power tended to derive from the possession of land. Support for those dubbed 'Whigs', however, came from the largely urban middle classes, who had grown rich from the investment and manipulation of capital – wealth understood as ready money rather than reposing in ancestral acres. Aptly, then, Whig and Tory interests were alternatively dubbed 'Town' and 'Country'.

The Tories had only reluctantly and belatedly supported the 'bloodless revolution' of 1688-89 and had kept their lines open to the deposed James, who was now exiled in France. This was one reason for the party's equivocation in the face of the wars against the French which dragged on through much of the 1690s, and which, renewed in 1701, form the background for *The Recruiting Officer*. Besides, the increased taxation necessitated by these wars weighed most heavily upon Tory supporters in the shires – whereas the profits from the munitions and materials consumed by the military tended to accrue to the Whig money-men in the City and their manufacturing allies.

The needs of the governing Whig regime for funds, and the exorbitant interest rates which its still-uncertain grip on power enabled the financiers to demand, had led in 1694 to the incorporation of the Bank of England: and this was followed four years later by the opening of the Stock Exchange. The Bank not only enjoyed monopoly powers but was authorised to make further loans on the security of the very money it raised for the government: and when the Bank began to issue credit notes, these quickly became (as they have remained) negotiable currency. However, the ever-mounting 'National Debt' created in the process would have been open to repudiation by a restored Jacobite line: thus, institutions founded to run the risks of supporting a shaky regime had a vested interest in consolidating the Whig constitutional settlement on which the economic confidence trick of 'paper-money' also depended.

Farquhar's early experiences in Ireland were clearly calculated to make him strong for the Whig cause, especially in pursuit of a war against the Catholic domination of Europe. He was thus among those Whigs whose militaristic fervour was rooted in patriotism rather than in party or commercial interests – and *The Recruiting Officer*, while satirising the excesses to which this could lead, is in part an attempt to transcend party differences by portraying a nation seemingly united in its support for the victorious allies.

Marlborough and the Military Background

The career of John Churchill, Duke of Marlborough, strikingly anticipated that of his distant descendant Winston. Both enjoyed early political success, suffered a period in eclipse (Winston's, in the 1930s, taken up with writing a four-volume biography of John), and returned to lead their country to military victory – only to see their party suffer political defeat, and to return to power in an old age blighted by physical infirmity.

Marlborough's early intimacy with the courts of Charles II and James II led (despite Marlborough's perhaps decisive desertion of the Jacobite cause) to his being viewed at first with suspicion by the new king. But William was slowly forced to acknowledge the Duke's military genius and designated Marlborough to succeed him as Commander-in-Chief of the Grand Alliance which had been formed by England, the Netherlands and Austria in 1700, when the grandson of Louis XIV succeeded to the Spanish throne.

Spain was especially prone to the French domination threatened by this development. Ironically, one source of the slow decline of Spanish power was the sheer size and unwieldiness of its empire – which included not only half of the New World, but also the Spanish Netherlands (roughly the equivalent of present-day Belgium) and a goodly portion of Italy besides. Louis's authoritarian rule, with its bureaucracy and social rigidity, was slowly but no less surely sapping

French pre-eminence in Europe: but this was less well recognised at the time, and from an early eighteenth-century perspective French power and influence seemed at a dangerous height. Louis gave further offence to the English when, on the death of the exiled James II in 1701, he recognised his son (remembered as 'the Old Pretender') as King of England. So the War of the Spanish Succession, fought nominally to assert the rights of an alternative, Austrian claimant to the Spanish throne, was no less calculated to thwart the restoration of the Stuart line in England.

France had seized the initiative by overrunning the Spanish Netherlands and Italy. Then William's death in 1702 saw Marlborough assume the allied command; a French advance on Vienna was reversed, and Marlborough's triumph at Blenheim followed in the August of 1704. This was not only a military victory, driving the French out of Germany, but a defining moment for the nation – the moment also of the composition and rehearsal of *The Recruiting Officer*. Party zealots apart, Whigs and Tories made common celebratory cause, and the play sees social classes, and the civil and military arm, united as seldom before or since. As Worthy says, in earlier wars, 'We had no blood nor wounds but in the officers' mouths . . . our officers did nothing but play at prison bars, and hide and seek with the enemy, but now ye have brought us colours and standards, and prisoners, odsmylife.' A grateful nation rewarded Marlborough by paying for the building of Blenheim Palace – designed by the architect and erstwhile dramatist, Sir John Vanbrugh.

The Recruiting Officer opened on 8 April 1706. Little over a month later came Marlborough's second great triumph, at Ramillies, which effectively secured the Netherlands, and later that year Prince Eugene's victory at Turin excluded the French from Italy. Thereafter, with the military issue only to be settled in the Netherlands, and the unrealistic diplomatic aim of getting Louis to relinquish support for his own grandson in Spain, support for the war declined, and by 1709 it was clear that its prolongation was serving the interests of the Whigs and their supporters rather than those of the nation at large.

The anti-war Tories at first claimed the support of the war leader Marlborough. But as the tide of patriotic fervour which followed Blenheim began to ebb, the Duke's fortunes became increasingly dependent on those of the war party – and when the Tories took power in 1710 English participation in the war was scaled down, and Marlborough dismissed from his command. The change in the national mood was reflected in a song interpolated between the acts of revivals of *The Recruiting Officer*, which glorified the generosity of Prince Eugene – and mocked the supposed stinginess of Marlborough.

Max Stafford-Clark (in *Letters to George*, a fascinating record of his own production of the play in 1988) laments that such 'plays of celebration' were never to be complemented by the 'plays of opposition' Farquhar might have written had he survived to see that Tory triumph, short-lived though it proved to be. It's an intriguing thought: but even had Farquhar been able to write such plays, they would have been banned – for one of the new Tory ministers, Bolingbroke, personally took on the task of assessing and censoring the drama.

The Recruiting Trade

In his authoritative history of Queen Anne's reign, G.M. Trevelyan tells us that between 1702 and 1709 the size of the English army rose from 18,000 to 70,000 men. Recruiting for an increase on this scale was clearly an activity vital to the national interest – and no less was it a highly topical subject for a play. Kite's list of wives (Act I, Scene i, p. 10) suggests the punishing itinerary he and his captain have been pursuing – having already seen active service at Blenheim. We get plentiful insights into the dubious tactics of the trade, such as the adding of an infant's name to the muster in order to draw his pay, and Farquhar shows us the suspicion with which its practitioners are viewed – whether in the 'Mob's' polite but firm rebuttal of Kite's blandishments in the first scene, or in the concern and humanity of Appletree's efforts to dissuade Pearmain before he reluctantly joins him (Act II, Scene iii, p. 33).

Farquhar dramatises both main forms of recruitment: voluntary enlistment, rewarded by a forty-shilling bounty (over a month's wages for a farm labourer); and 'impressment' by compulsion of 'such able-bodied men as have not any lawful calling or employment, or visible means for their maintenance and livelihood'. Such 'pressed' recruits got only twenty shillings, ten more going to the constable who rounded them up – hence the eleven shillings that, in actuality as well as in the play, often sufficed to outbid the law.

And so, as Farquhar's editor Peter Dixon reminds us, 'There is a grim reality behind Costar's joke that, thanks to the pressing act, justices are "greater than any emperor under the sun".' As for the prospects of greatness and nobility held out by Kite to such taproom rustics, the Sergeant's own potted autobiography in Act III, Scene i (p. 38) confirms that he is condemned by his humble origins to remain unpromoted (it took the disasters of the Crimea, 150 years later, even to nibble at the class privilege on which a commission depended in the British army).

Nobody in *The Recruiting Officer* actually enlists without being either hoodwinked or reluctantly impressed – the only apparently willing volunteer, Jack Wilful, being of course a fraud. And in practice few justices of the Tory shires were – despite the reservations of Scale and (especially) Scruple – as co-operative with the military as were those of Farquhar's Shrewsbury, where every rule is bent in favour of impressment. Farquhar was sufficiently a realist to know that the rural magistracy was more often concerned at the depletion of its civilian troops of farm workers, day labourers, and household servants than with the advancement of a safely distant and dubiously motivated war. The patriotic muting of such reservations in the aftermath of Blenheim proved a temporary phenomenon.

The Scene: Shrewsbury

Tradition has it that Farquhar wrote *The Recruiting Officer* at the Raven Inn in Shrewsbury, the county town of Shropshire on the Welsh border, where he sets his play. This would presumably have been in the second half of 1705, at some time after his own recruiting activities were removed here from Lichfield (the setting he later used for *The Beaux Stratagem*). A contemporary resident, recalling the visit some sixty years later, was able to come up with real-life originals for the play's main characters: but such source-spotting, seldom very helpful to our understanding, is least so when all that has survived of these 'originals' is what Farquhar chose to filter out.

More pertinent, perhaps, are the observations on the town made by Daniel Defoe – a devious politician (engaged in 1706 in spying out the land for the imminent Act of Union with Scotland) long before he became better known to us as the author of such proto-novels as

Robinson Crusoe. In his *Tour through the Whole Island of Great Britain*, Defoe recalls that Shrewsbury had suffered during the Commonwealth for its welcome to Charles I before the Battle of Edgehill: but by the time of Defoe's *Tour*, in the early 1720s, it was 'one of the most flourishing towns in England . . . full of gentry and yet full of trade too', with 'the greatest plenty of good provisions, and the cheapest that is to be met with in all the western part of England'. This, he says, 'draws a great many families hither, who love to live within the compass of their estates' – after the manner of Justice Balance, who settles himself in his town house for the winter 'season', but remains within easy reach of his country residence, where he thinks it will be expedient to seclude his daughter.

Like a horse-shoe, according to Defoe, the Severn 'surrounds this town, just as the Thames does the Isle of Dogs'. The riverside of *The Recruiting Officer* is not a rustic retreat, but a fashionable urban place of resort – more akin to St James's Park than the Isle of Dogs in Restoration London. Shrewsbury is 'really a town of mirth and gallantry' – perhaps a double-edged compliment from the nonconformist Defoe, who was not much given to either. Against this contemporary view, Farquhar has Worthy complaining to Plume that 'We live in such a precise, dull place, that we can have no balls, no lampoons', and Melinda grumbling to Silvia that here is 'every thing to give the spleen, and nothing to divert it'.

For Farquhar's London audience, remarks such as these affirmed the Restoration belief in the superiority of town over country – yet most modern critics share with Eric Rothstein a contrary impression, that 'Shrewsbury values are the normative values of the play'. In this respect, it is perhaps helpful to remember that only recently Farquhar had himself been a stranger in London: at first overawed by its attractions, he was unsure of his social bearings when he so speedily joined its circle of sophisticates – and all the more dismayed when his early success turned sour. Shrewsbury and Lichfield must have revealed a culture he had not previously suspected – its rich diversity likely to prove sympathetic to the sensibility of this young Irishman in exile. Yet as a practising dramatist Farquhar could not afford to espouse values too much at variance with those of the London audiences who would determine his play's success. And so, while Restoration plays had been written *for* (and often from within) the

Court, and *against* the despised 'cits' and others beyond the charmed circle of the social elite, Farquhar is writing *for* and *with* the 'country', defined not as a primitive 'other' but as part of the nation state whose military achievements he is celebrating.

Characters and Character Types

In *The Recruiting Officer* there are echoes of Restoration 'typology' – the moulding of characters into the conventionalised social types of the comedy of manners – in such carefully contrasted 'gallants' as Worthy and Plume. There are Elizabethan and Jacobean resonances, too: Brazen's genealogical obsession is a typical Jonsonian 'humour', or affectation, while Silvia's male disguise and Kite's verbal dexterity are more indebted to Shakespearean precedent – recalling, respectively, Rosalind in *As You Like It* and Touchstone in *Twelfth Night*.

And all the characters owe something to the actors Farquhar had in mind for them. As Peter Dixon reminds us, of the company which first performed *The Recruiting Officer* not only Wilks, tailor-made for Plume, but Estcourt as Kite, Keen as Balance, and Norris as Pearmain had all been with the Smock Alley company in Dublin before Farquhar had worked with them in London. And, having already in *The Twin Rivals* tested the muscles of that canny actor-manager-cum-dramatist Colley Cibber in parts beyond his usual modish fops, Farquhar here further extended Cibber's range in the role of Brazen.

Brazen's ancestry is complex. Although in part the jaded gallant, he can also trace his lineage to the 'braggart soldier' of classical comedy, and blends the affectations of his fellow-captain, Bobadill, in Jonson's *Every Man in His Humour* with those of Sir Politic in *Volpone* – no less dedicated a collector of ill-considered trifles. Yet Brazen is also his own man – displaying, as in Laurence Olivier's performance of 1964, a distinctive combination of chronic vagueness and reluctant valour. Unlike so many of his Restoration forebears, it seems, too, that Brazen really *does* have the wide acquaintance he claims: his intimate knowledge of Balance's uncle and brother in the last scene could scarcely have been feigned.

The now complacent, domestically benign but judicially severe Balance sees in Plume his younger self: and Plume treads a dramatic tightrope between his profession, his social position, his theatrical lineage, and the individuality with which he was endowed by both his creators – second to Farquhar being, of course, Robert Wilks, who had earlier ensured that Wildair lived up to his name. Earlier Restoration officers – from the title characters in Otway's *Soldiers' Fortune* to Farquhar's own Colonel Standard in *The Constant Couple* – had been disbanded before their first entrances: yet such antecedents remind us that the army was the one career which could honourably be pursued by a gentleman – a class otherwise distinguished by the pursuit of leisure.

Although Plume displays a self-assurance that comes close to vanity – not only as a master of his gentlemanly profession, but in his complacent offer to stand in for Worthy in the winning of Melinda – he also has a spontaneous generosity seldom found in his calculating forebears. His gesture of foregoing the money he was about to demand for Silvia's discharge anticipates (say) the refusal of Charles Surface in Sheridan's *The School for Scandal* to part with the picture of his uncle. In both cases the effect is to persuade a sceptical elder of intrinsic good nature – a quality which was to stand in opposition to sentimentalised and often hypocritical 'virtue' through much of the eighteenth century.

Melinda and Worthy, too, can be seen as early types of the sentimental couple, as gently parodied in the characters of Julia and Faulkland in Sheridan's *The Rivals* – though the role of a pair of 'serious' lovers to counterpoise the 'gay couple' is reminiscent of Shakespeare's balancing of Hero and Claudio against Beatrice and Benedick in *Much Ado About Nothing*. But here too Farquhar transcends mere typology. As Max Stafford-Clark suggests: 'Melinda's fiery vindictiveness and determination to punish Worthy is not just the flighty behaviour of a soubrette, it is the pre-feminist bitterness of a young woman who has seen the abyss into which she has nearly been tumbled.' Angellica Bianca in Aphra Behn's *The Rover* offers a role-model for the profession of courtesan that was a woman's only independent option once she had become a cast-off mistress: and Melinda has something of her strength.

Kite is an original – and although several critics suggest that the Sergeant works the same line in flexible confidence-trickery as Face and Subtle in *The Alchemist*, that is to miss the point that Jonson's fraudsters are operating on their own behalf. Kite (with only a then quite usual expectation of backhanders) instead works hard on behalf of his Captain and, indeed (as he and his age would see it), his country. In his ingenuity and verbal dexterity he rather resembles the Elizabethan clown – even down to his acceptance of being beaten and humbled as an occupational hazard.

Silvia, played by Farquhar's protégée Anne Oldfield, sustains a long tradition of theatrical cross-dressing. In Elizabethan drama young women, played by young boys, often found occasion (as does Rosalind in *As You Like It*) to don a male 'disguise'. With the Restoration, actresses could wear their own 'breeches', to the evident delight of audiences who relished the mild titillation. And Silvia's tomboy qualities are mentioned several times before she assumes her disguise – Melinda even ironically remarking that Silvia 'begins to fancy yourself in breeches in good earnest' (Act I, Scene ii, p. 18). Already, Farquhar had put Leanthe in *Love and a Bottle*, Angelica in *The Constant Couple*, and Oriana in *The Inconstant* into breeches – and this was, indeed, one of the few ways in which a dramatist could allow a young woman to assert her independence of her father or to take the initiative with a lover.

Love and War, Contracts and Cash

It is not fashionable these days to pin down the 'themes' of plays: 'meaning', according to many modern critics, cannot be imposed, but is a matter for each individual reader (as actors and audiences, making meaning anew with each new production, discovered long ago). It is none the less worth noting the observation of Farquhar's editor John Ross that the themes of love and war are here ironically intertwined: the twin love-plots are replete with references to sieges and blockades, while recruiting is portrayed as a process of either seducing men into the service or of enforcing unwilling complicity.

Not so much a theme as a recurrent motif in the play is Farquhar's concern with contracts and other forms of agreement – from the propriety of recruiting tactics and the grounds for impressment or its evasion to the genuineness or otherwise of signatures on bits of paper, whether on Plume's will in favour of Silvia, made on the eve of Blenheim, or in Melinda's letters of varied provenance.

Marriage contracts or their anticipation are also a central concern. We know exactly how much Silvia is 'worth', both before and after her brother's death, and no less precisely that Worthy was prepared to settle £500 a year on Melinda as his mistress. This was a very considerable sum (Farquhar's father is said to have kept his family on £150), but of course it was on offer only because she was too poor to be made an honest woman – for it is her inheritance of £20,000 that now makes her a suitable match. There is also the clear suggestion that if Melinda had not held out against Worthy's 'artful baits' and 'cunning pretences', he might not have come up with the cash. When Melinda finally consents, it is to balance one 'account' against the other, and so 'begin a new score'.

There are military contracts, too: notably (and twice read aloud) the Articles of War, by which death is the punishment for almost any transgression – including of course desertion, although we are evidently supposed to view Plume's climactic abandonment of his commission as both morally and dramatically acceptable. Bill Gaskill's production in 1964 contrasted Plume's casual resignation with the irretrievable commitment of his recruits, culling from a military treatise of the times a final speech for Brazen as he leads off his hand-me-down band: 'Soldiers, look lively! Take care of your exercise, bearing your arms well, and keeping due time.'

Farquhar also shows us the Game Laws operating in the class interests of the squirarchy. As Rose tells us in Act III, Scene i (p. 42), she has often seen Balance hunting across her father's farm – for game to which her father as tenant had no rights. Yet Balance is quite prepared to impress into the service a poacher from the lower orders, who shoots hares and partridge only to feed his family. In such matters of contemporary class warfare, Farquhar is an accurate observer without, it appears, being overly critical.

As a last reflection on contemporary attitudes, we might note that the 'contract' between nations which in 1714 formally ended the War of the Spanish Succession – and which settled the shape of Europe for over seventy years – gave England a monopoly in supplying the Spanish Americas with an essential 'commodity': human slaves.

The Theatre of Farquhar's London

Looking back nostalgically from 1725 to the time when play-acting returned to London with the Restoration (after being banned by the puritans since 1642), John Dennis remarked that 'They alter'd at once the whole face of the stage by introducing scenes and women.' This was not quite true: the court masques of the Jacobean and Caroline period had employed scenery, and the open-air theatres of the Elizabethans had long been giving way to indoor 'private' theatres, with greater potential for technical effects. The difference now was that the proscenium arch formed a 'picture-frame' for the perspective scenery painted onto 'wings and shutters', which provided a formalized background to Restoration plays in performance.

But it was *only* a background: for the actors played in front of the proscenium on an ample apron stage – in a relationship with their audiences no less intimate and uncluttered than that of their forebears. Indeed, Restoration theatres, which seated from around five to eight hundred, were considerably smaller than the Elizabethan public playhouses, and their audiences, although not drawn quite so exclusively from a courtly elite as is sometimes claimed, did feel themselves to be part of a social as much as of a theatrical occasion.

Royal patents limited playing to two companies of fewer than thirty apiece: so acting was an exclusive though not prestigious profession, its members as well-known personally to many in the audience as their own acquaintances in the pit or boxes. Following the alleged 'Popish Plot' of 1678, with practical politics increasingly distracting the attention of the courtly audiences, the two companies actually joined forces – the Drury Lane company alone sufficing to serve London's theatregoers from 1682 to 1695. Then Thomas Betterton, the leading player of his generation, quarrelled with the manager at Drury Lane, and took a group of actors to the playhouse in Lincoln's Inn Fields – and the ensuing 'warfare' between the two houses was in full swing when Farquhar's first play, *Love and a Bottle*, reached the stage in December 1698.

It might have seemed that Farquhar, in entrusting this play to Drury Lane, would be on the losing side, for Betterton had taken with him the best-known players of the day, including the leading actresses Elizabeth Barry and Anne Bracegirdle – and the opening production there, of Congreve's *Love for Love*, had set a sparkling standard. But as Colley Cibber, one of the younger players at Drury Lane, put it in his autobiography, the *Apology*, 'Betterton's people . . . were most of them too far advanc'd in years to mend; and tho' we, in Drury Lane, were too young to be excellent, we were not too old to be better.' Such luminaries of the new generation as Susannah Verbruggen and William Pinkethman had thus remained loyal, and over the next few years were joined by William Bullock, Farquhar's friends Robert Wilks and Henry Norris, and the beautiful young actress destined to create the role of Silvia, his admired Anne Oldfield.

Cibber's proto-sentimental *Love's Last Shift* had been the outstanding success of 1696 at Drury Lane, to be followed by Vanbrugh's comic sequel, *The Relapse*, in 1697 – then, in 1699, the achievement by Farquhar of over fifty performances of *The Constant Couple* in its first season set the seal on the younger company's ascendancy. Although Farquhar took *The Stage-Coach* to Lincoln's Inn Fields in 1703, he otherwise remained loyal to the Drury Lane company – and they to him, through this problematic period – and it was here that *The Recruiting Officer* was so happily received in April 1706.

In the autumn of that year, however, a number of the now rising players defected to the new Queen's theatre in the Haymarket, which had housed Betterton's company since its opening in the previous year. This playhouse had been designed and was briefly managed by Sir John Vanbrugh – who in 1705 had received the commission to build Blenheim Palace, and wrote his last completed play, *The Mistake*, for the Queen's company in December. Farquhar contributed a prologue to the first production of the new season, and it was here that his own last play, *The Beaux Stratagem*, opened in March 1707.

In the event, this was to be one of the very few successes at a play-house whose acoustics made it unsuitable for the spoken drama. By 1708, it was given over to opera, and the actors had returned to Drury Lane, where (after a few further vicissitudes) a new manage-ment, including Cibber and Wilks, inaugurated a period of relative stability – albeit, owing in part to Farquhar's premature death and the censorship of the new Tory government, one of sparse and lack-lustre new writing.

A Note on the Text and Punctuation

The following text of *The Recruiting Officer* is based on the first edition, which was published in late April 1706, hard on the heels of the first performance of the play (the errors introduced into the second edition outweigh its allegedly 'corrected' state, and the changes it incorporates are more often pedantic than dramatic). Speeches assigned to the Mob in Act II, Scene iii, have been distributed here between Pearmain and Appletree, as indicated by their context.

In the interests of clarity and series style, certain conventions of eighteenth-century typography have been modernised in this edition: thus, the italicising of proper names and the surfeit of initial capitalisation have alike been silently modified. Speech headings and the positioning of stage directions have also been regularised. Spelling has been more cautiously updated, since the original form can often be helpful in suggesting pronunciation or stress.

In his *Discourse upon Comedy*, Farquhar had discussed the need of the comic form to employ the 'natural air of free conversation': and his dialogue in *The Recruiting Officer* employs the rhetoric of speech rather than of the written word. The original punctuation has, therefore, been retained – notably, Farquhar's use of the dash, a useful indication of that rhetorical catching of the breath which may or as often may not coincide with a more regular mark of punctuation. Our modern tendency, even in playtexts, to make punctuation accord with grammatical useage is a legacy of the later eighteenth-century desire for 'correctness', and reflects Latinate rules rather than what regulates pauses and emphases in the way people actually speak.

Simon Trussler

For Further Reading

Critical writing on Farquhar includes A. J. Farmer's introductory pamphlet in the 'Writers and Their Work' series (London: Longmans, for the British Council, 1966); Eric Rothstein's more detailed study in the 'Twayne's English Authors' series (New York: Twayne, 1967); and Eugene N. James's *The Development of Farquhar as a Comic Dramatist* (The Hague: Mouton, 1972), which is both more advanced and often more contentious. A sampling of shorter essays on the *The Recruiting Officer* and *The Beaux Stratagem* can be found in the Macmillan 'Casebook' series, edited by Raymond A. Anselment (1977). The only biography, now rather out-of-date, is Willard Connely's *Young George Farquhar* (Cassell, 1949).

Max Stafford-Clark's *Letters to George: the Account of a Rehearsal* (London: Nick Hern Books, 1989) is an articulate and accessible record of rehearsals for the Royal Court production of *The Recruiting Officer* in 1988. Bill Gaskill's seminal National Theatre production of 1964 is less amply served by the text-cum-commentary edited by Kenneth Tynan (Hart-Davis, 1965). Thomas Keneally's *The Playmaker* (London: Hodder and Stoughton, 1987) is an absorbing fictional account of a much earlier production, in 1789 – when *The Recruiting Officer* was the first play ever performed in Australia, by settlers in a penal colony.

For the more advanced student, modern editions of *The Recruiting Officer* have appeared in the Regents Restoration Drama series, edited by Michael Shugrue (Arnold, 1965), the New Mermaid series, edited by John Ross (Benn, 1973 and 1991), and the Revels Plays series, edited by Peter Dixon (Manchester UP, 1986). A new critical edition of Farquhar's *Works*, edited by Shirley Strum Kenny, was published in 1988 by Oxford University Press. Among more broadly-based works, Jocelyn Powell's *Restoration Theatre Production* (Routledge, 1984) is recommended for its investigation of acting style and conventions, and Peter Holland's *The Ornament of Action* (Cambridge, 1979) for its discussion of the relationship between text and performance.

Farquhar: Key Dates

1677 *c.* Born in Londonderry.

1689 Presumably still in Londonderry during the Jacobite siege. Volunteered to fight in the Battle of the Boyne in 1690?

1694 Entered Trinity College, Dublin, as a 'sizar' – receiving scant board and tuition in return for menial duties.

1696 Left Trinity College without his degree, and acted at the Smock Alley Theatre in Dublin, making his debut as Othello.

1697 Left for London to try his fortune as a playwright.

1698 *Love and a Bottle* (published 1699), Drury Lane, December.

1699 *The Constant Couple* (published 1700), Drury Lane, November.

1701 *Sir Harry Wildair,* Drury Lane, April, and published.

1702 *The Inconstant* (published 1702) and *The Twin-Rivals* (published 1703), both Drury Lane.

1703 Marriage to Margaret Pemell. *The Stage-Coach* (published 1704), Lincoln's Inn Fields, December (or January 1704).

1704 Commissioned as a Lieutenant of Grenadiers. Birth of his first daughter, Anne Marguerite.

1705 On recruiting service in Lichfield and Shrewsbury. Birth of his second daughter, Mary.

1706 *The Recruiting Officer,* Drury Lane, April, and published. Farquhar was already ill, presumably with tuberculosis.

1707 *The Beaux Stratagem,* Haymarket, March, and published. Farquhar now gravely ill. He died in May, in his thirtieth year, in a 'back garret' in St. Martin's Lane.

THE RECRUITING OFFICER

Epistle Dedicatory

My Lords and Gentlemen,

Instead of the mercenary expectations that attend addresses of this nature, I humbly beg, that this may be received as an acknowledgement for the favours you have already conferr'd; I have transgress'd the Rules of Dedication in offering you any thing in that style, without first asking your leave: but the entertainment I found in Shropshire commands me to be grateful, and that's all I intend.

'Twas my good fortune to be order'd some time ago into the place which is made the scene of this comedy; I was a perfect stranger to everything in Salop, but its character of loyalty, the number of its inhabitants, the alacrity of the gentlemen in recruiting the army, with their generous and hospitable reception of strangers.

This character I found so amply verified in every particular, that you made recruiting, which is the greatest fatigue upon earth to others, to be the greatest pleasure in the world to me.

The kingdom cannot show better bodies of men, better inclinations for the service, more generosity, more good understanding, nor more politeness than is to be found at the foot of the Wrekin.

Some little turns of humour that I met with almost within the shade of that famous hill, gave the rise to this comedy; and people were apprehensive, that, by the example of some others, I would make the town merry at the expense of the country gentlemen: but they forgot that I was to write a comedy, not a libel; and that whilst I held to nature, no person of any character in your country could suffer by being expos'd. I have drawn the justice and the clown in their *puris naturalibus:* the one an apprehensive, sturdy, brave blockhead, and the other a worthy, honest, generous gentleman, hearty in his country's cause, and of as good an understanding as I could give him, which I must confess is far short of his own.

I humbly beg leave to interline a word or two of the adventures of the *Recruiting Officer* upon the stage. Mr. Rich, who commands the company for which those recruits were rais'd, has desir'd me to acquit him before the world of a charge which he thinks lies heavy upon him for acting this play on Mr. Durfey's third night.

Be it known unto all men by these presents, that it was my act and deed, or rather Mr. Durfey's; for he *would* play his third night against the first of mine. He brought down a huge flight of frightful birds upon me, when (Heaven knows) I had not a feather'd fowl in my play, except one single Kite: but I presently made Plume a bird, because of his name, and Brazen another, because of the feather in his hat; and with these three I engag'd his whole empire, which I think was as great a wonder as any in the Sun.

But to answer his complaints more gravely, the season was far advanc'd; the officers that made the greatest figures in my play were all commanded to their posts abroad, and waited only for a wind, which might possibly turn in less time than a day: and I know none of Mr. Durfey's birds that had posts abroad but his woodcocks, and their season is over; so that he might put off a day with less prejudice than the *Recruiting Officer* could, who has this farther to say for himself, that he was posted before the other spoke, and could not with credit recede from his station.

These and some other rubs this comedy met with before it appear'd. But on the other hand, it had powerful helps to set it forward: the Duke of Ormonde encourag'd the author, and the Earl of Orrery approv'd the play – my recruits were reviewed by my General and my Colonel, and could not fail to pass muster; and still to add to my success, they were rais'd among my friends round the Wrekin.

This health has the advantage over our other celebrated toasts, never to grow worse for the wearing: 'tis a lasting beauty, old without age and common without scandal. That you may live long to set it cheerfully round, and to enjoy the abundant pleasures of your fair and plentiful country, is the hearty wish of,

> *My Lords and Gentlemen,* your most obliged, and most obedient
> servant, *Geo. Farquhar*

The Prologue

In ancient times, when Helen's fatal charms
Roused the contending universe to arms,
The Græcian council happily deputes
The sly Ulysses forth – to raise recruits.
The artful captain found, without delay,
Where great Achilles, a deserter, lay.
Him Fate had warn'd to shun the Trojan blows:
Him Greece requir'd – against their Trojan foes.
All the recruiting arts were needful here
To raise this great, this tim'rous volunteer.
Ulysses well could talk – He stirs, he warms
The warlike youth – He listens to the charms
Of plunder, fine lac'd coats, and glitt'ring arms.
Ulysses caught the young aspiring boy,
And listed him who wrought the fate of Troy.
Thus by recruiting was bold Hector slain;
Recruiting thus fair Helen did regain.
If for one Helen such prodigious things
Were acted, that they ev'n listed kings;
If for one Helen's artful vicious charms,
Half the transported world was found in arms;.
What for so many Helens may *we* dare,
Whose minds, as well as faces, are so fair?
If, by one Helen's eyes, old Greece could find
Its Homer fir'd to write – ev'n Homer blind;
The Britons sure beyond compare may write,
That view so many Helens every night.

Dramatis Personae

MR. BALANCE
MR. SCALE
MR. SCRUPLE, *three Justices*
MR. WORTHY, *a gentleman of Shropshire*
CAPTAIN PLUME
CAPTAIN BRAZEN, *two recruiting officers*
KITE, *Sergeant to Plume*
BULLOCK, *a country clown*
COSTAR PEARMAIN
THOMAS APPLETREE, *two recruits*
PLUCK, *a butcher*
THOMAS, *a smith*
BRIDEWELL, *a constable*

WOMEN

MELINDA, *a lady of fortune*
SILVIA, *daughter to Balance, in love with Plume*
LUCY, *Melinda's maid*
ROSE, *a country wench*

Recruits, Mob, Servants and Attendants.

Scene, *Shrewsbury.*

Act I, Scene i

Scene, the market-place – drum beats the Grenadier-March. Enter SERGEANT KITE, *followed by the* MOB.

KITE (*making a speech*). If any gentlemen soldiers, or others, have a mind to serve Her Majesty, and pull down the French King; if any prentices have severe masters, any children have undutiful parents; if any servants have too little wages, or any husband too much wife; let them repair to the noble Sergeant Kite, at the Sign of the Raven, in this good town of Shrewsbury, and they shall receive present relief and entertainment. –

Gentlemen, I don't beat my drums here to ensnare or inveigle any man; for you must know, gentlemen, that I am a man of honour: besides, I don't beat up for common soldiers; no, I list only grenadiers, grenadiers, gentlemen – Pray, gentlemen, observe this cap – this is the cap of honour, it dubs a man a gentleman in the drawing of a tricker; and he that has the good fortune to be born six foot high, was born to be a great man. – Sir, (*To one of the* MOB.) will you give me leave to try this cap upon your head?

MOB. Is there no harm in 't? Won't the cap list me?

KITE. No, no, no more than I can, – come, let me see how it becomes you.

MOB. Are you sure there be no conjuration in it, no gunpowder-plot upon me?

KITE. – No, no, friend; don't fear, man.

MOB. My mind misgives me plaguely – let me see it. (*Going to put it on.*) It smells woundily of sweat and brimstone; pray, Sergeant, what writing is this upon the face of it?

KITE. The Crown, or the Bed of Honour.

MOB. Pray now, what may be that same Bed of Honour?

KITE. Oh, a mighty large bed, bigger by half than the great bed of Ware, ten thousand people may lie in 't together and never feel one another.

MOB. My wife and I would do well to lie in 't, for we don't care for feeling one another – but do folk sleep sound in this same Bed of Honour?

KITE. Sound! Aye, so sound that they never wake.

MOB. Wauns! I wish again that my wife lay there.

KITE. Say you so? Then I find brother –

MOB. Brother! Hold there, friend, I'm no kindred to you that I know of, as yet – Look ye, Sergeant, no coaxing, no wheedling, d' ye see; if I have a mind to list, why so – if not, why 'tis not so – therefore take your cap and your brothership back again, for I an't disposed at this present writing – no coaxing, no brothering me, faith.

KITE. I coax! I wheedle! I'm above it. Sir, I have serv'd twenty campaigns. – But sir, you talk well, and I must own that you are a man every inch of you, a pretty young sprightly fellow – I love a fellow with a spirit, but I scorn to coax, 'tis base; tho' I must say that never in my life have I seen a better built man: how firm and strong he treads, he steps like a castle! But I scorn to wheedle any man – come, honest lad, will you take share of a pot?

MOB. Nay, for that matter, I'll spend my penny with the best he that wears a head, that is, begging your pardon, sir, and in a fair way.

KITE. Give me your hand then; and now, gentlemen, I have no more to say but this – here's a purse of gold, and there is a tub of humming ale at my quarters, 'tis the Queen's money, and the Queen's drink; she's a generous Queen, and loves her subjects – I hope, gentlemen, you won't refuse the Queen's health.

ALL MOB. No, no, no.

KITE. Huzza then, huzza for the Queen, and the honour of Shropshire!

ALL MOB. Huzza!

KITE. Beat drum –

Exeunt, drummer beating the 'Grenadier March'.

Enter PLUME *in a riding habit.*

PLUME. By the 'Grenadier-March' that should be my drum, and by that shout it should beat with success – Let me see – (*Looks on his watch.*) – four o'clock – at ten yesterday morning I left London – a hundred and twenty miles in thirty hours, is pretty smart riding, but nothing to the fatigue of recruiting.

Enter KITE.

KITE. Welcome to Shrewsbury, noble Captain, from the banks of the Danube to the Severn side, noble Captain, you are welcome.

PLUME. A very elegant reception indeed, Mr. Kite, I find you are fairly enter'd into your recruiting strain – pray, what success?

KITE. I have been here but a week, and I have recruited five.

PLUME. Five! Pray, what are they?

KITE. I have listed the strong man of Kent, the King of the Gypsies, a Scotch pedlar, a scoundrel attorney, and a Welsh parson.

PLUME. An attorney! Wert thou mad? List a lawyer! Discharge him, discharge him this minute.

KITE. Why, sir?

PLUME. Because I will have no body in my company that can write; a fellow that can write, can draw petitions – I say, this minute discharge him.

KITE. And what shall I do with the parson?

PLUME. Can he write?

KITE. Umh – he plays rarely upon the fiddle.

PLUME. Keep him by all means – But how stands the country affected? Were the people pleas'd with the news of my coming to town?

KITE. Sir, the mob are so pleased with your honour, and the justices and better sort of people are so delighted with me, that we shall soon do our business – But, sir, you have got a recruit here that you little think of.

PLUME. Who?

KITE. One that you beat up for last time you were in the country; you remember your old friend Molly at the Castle?

PLUME. She's not with child, I hope.

KITE. No, no, sir; she was brought to bed yesterday.

PLUME. Kite, you must father the child.

KITE. Humph – and so her friends will oblige me to marry the mother.

PLUME. If she should, we'll take her with us, she can wash, you know, and make a bed upon occasion.

KITE. Aye, or unmake it upon occasion, but your honour knows that I'm married already.

PLUME. To how many?

KITE. I can't tell readily – I have set them down here upon the back of the muster-roll. (*Draws it out.*) Let me see – *Imprimis*, Mrs. Sheely Snickereyes, she sells potatoes upon Ormonde Quay in Dublin – Peggy Guzzle, the brandy-woman at the Horse-guard at Whitehall – Dolly Waggon, the carrier's daughter in Hull – Madamoiselle Van-Bottomflat at the Buss – then Jenny Okam, the ship-carpenter's widow at Portsmouth, but I don't reckon upon her, for she was married at the same time to two lieutenants of marines, and a man of war's boatswain.

PLUME. A full company – you have named five – come, make 'em half a dozen, Kite – is the child a boy or a girl?

KITE. A chopping boy.

PLUME. Then set the mother down in your list, and the boy in mine: enter him a grenadier by the name of Francis Kite, absent upon furlough – I'll allow you a man's pay for his subsistence, and now go comfort the wench in the straw.

KITE. I shall, sir.

PLUME. But hold, have you made any use of your German doctor's habit since you arriv'd?

KITE. Yes, yes, sir; and my fame's all about the country for the most faithful fortune-teller that ever told a lie; I was oblig'd to let my landlord into the secret for the convenience of keeping it so, but he's an honest fellow, and will be trusty to any roguery that is confided to him. This device, sir, will get you men, and me money, which I think is all we want at present – But yonder comes your friend Mr. Worthy – Has your honour any farther commands?

PLUME. None at present.

Exit KITE.

'Tis indeed the picture of Worthy, but the life's departed.

Enter WORTHY.

PLUME. What! Arms a-cross, Worthy! Methinks you should hold 'em open when a friend's so near – The man has got the vapours in his ears, I believe. I must expel this melancholy spirit.

> *Spleen, thou worst of fiends below,*
> *Fly, I conjure thee by this magic blow.*

Slaps WORTHY *on the shoulder.*

WORTHY. Plume! My dear Captain, welcome, safe and sound return'd!

PLUME. I 'scap'd safe from Germany, and sound, I hope, from London, you see I have lost neither leg, arm, nor nose – Then for my inside, 'tis neither troubled with sympathies nor antipathies, and I have an excellent stomach for roast beef.

WORTHY. Thou art a happy fellow, once I was so.

PLUME. What ails thee, man? No inundations nor earthquakes in Wales, I hope? Has your father rose from the dead, and reassum'd his estate?

WORTHY. No.

PLUME. Then, you are married surely.

WORTHY. No.

PLUME. Then you are mad, or turning Quaker.

WORTHY. Come, I must out with it – Your once gay roving friend is dwindled into an obsequious, thoughtful, romantic, constant coxcomb.

PLUME. And pray, what is all this for?

WORTHY. For a woman.

PLUME. Shake hands, brother, if you go to that – behold me as obsequious, as thoughtful, and as constant a coxcomb as your worship.

WORTHY. For whom?

PLUME. For a regiment. – But for a woman, 'sdeath, I have been constant to fifteen at a time, but never melancholy for one; and can the love of one bring you into this pickle? Pray, who is this miraculous Helen?

WORTHY. A Helen indeed, not to be won under a ten years' siege, as great a beauty, and as great a jilt.

PLUME. A jilt! Pho – Is she as great a whore?

WORTHY. No, no.

PLUME. 'Tis ten thousand pities – But who is she? Do I know her?

WORTHY. Very well.

PLUME. Impossible! – I know no woman that will hold out a ten years' siege.

WORTHY. What think you of Melinda?

PLUME. Melinda! Why, she began to capitulate this time twelve-month, and offer'd to surrender upon honourable terms; and I advis'd you to propose a settlement of five hundred pound a year to her, before I went last abroad.

WORTHY. I did, and she hearken'd to 't, desiring only one week to consider; when, beyond her hopes, the town was reliev'd, and I forc'd to turn my siege into a blockade.

PLUME. Explain, explain.

WORTHY. My Lady Richly her aunt in Flintshire dies, and leaves her at this critical time twenty thousand pound.

PLUME. Oh the devil, what a delicate woman was there spoil'd! But by the rules of war now, Worthy, blockade was foolish – After such a convoy of provisions was entered the place, you could have no thought of reducing it by famine – you should have redoubled your attacks, taken the town by storm, or have died upon the breach.

WORTHY. I did make one general assault, and pushed it with all my forces; but I was so vigorously repuls'd, that despairing of ever gaming her for a mistress, I have alter'd my conduct, given my addresses the obsequious and distant turn, and court her now for a wife.

PLUME. So, as you grew obsequious, she grew haughty, and because you approach'd her as a goddess, she us'd you like a dog.

WORTHY. Exactly.

PLUME. 'Tis the way of 'em all – Come Worthy, your obsequious and distant airs will never bring you together; you must not think to surmount her pride by your humility – Would you bring her to better thoughts of you, she must be reduc'd to a meaner opinion of herself – Let me see – The very first thing that I would do, should be to lie with her chamber-maid, and hire three or four wenches in the neighbourhood to report that I had got them with child. Suppose we lampoon'd all the pretty women in town, and left her out? Or what if we made a ball, and forgot to invite her, with one or two of the ugliest?

WORTHY. These would be mortifications, I must confess; but we live in such a precise, dull place that we can have no balls, no lampoons, no –

PLUME. What! No bastards! And so many recruiting officers in town; I thought 'twas a maxim among them to leave as many recruits in the country as they carried out.

WORTHY. No body doubts your good-will, noble Captain, in serving your country with your best blood – Witness our friend

Molly at the Castle – there have been tears in town about that business, Captain.

PLUME. I hope Silvia has not heard of 't.

WORTHY. Oh sir, have you thought of her? I began to fancy you had forgot poor Silvia.

PLUME. Your affairs had put mine quite out of my head. 'Tis true, Silvia and I had once agreed to go to bed together, could we have adjusted preliminaries; but she would have the wedding before consummation, and I was for consummation before the wedding – we could not agree. She was a pert obstinate fool, and would lose her maidenhead her own way, so she may keep it for Plume.

WORTHY. But do you intend to marry upon no other conditions?

PLUME. Your pardon, sir, I'll marry upon no condition at all, if I should, I'm resolv'd never to bind myself to a woman for my whole life, till I know whether I shall like her company for half an hour – Suppose I married a woman that wanted a leg? Such a thing might be, unless I examin'd the goods beforehand; if people would but try one another's constitutions before they engag'd, it would prevent all these elopements, divorces, and the devil knows what.

WORTHY. Nay, for that matter, the town did not stick to say, that –

PLUME. I hate country towns for that reason – If your town has a dishonourable thought of Silvia, it deserves to be burnt to the ground – I love Silvia, I admire her frank, generous disposition; there's something in that girl more than woman, her sex is but a foil to her – The ingratitude, dissimulation, envy, pride, avarice, and vanity of her sister females, do but set off their contraries in her – in short, were I once a general, I would marry her.

WORTHY. Faith you have reason; for were you but a corporal, she would marry you – But my Melinda coquettes it with every fellow she sees – I lay fifty pound she makes love to you.

PLUME I'll lay fifty pound that I return it, if she does – Look 'ee, Worthy, I'll win her, and give her to you afterwards.

WORTHY. If you win her, you shall wear her, faith; I would not give a fig for the conquest, without the credit of the victory.

Enter KITE.

KITE. Captain, Captain, a word in your ear.

PLUME. You may speak out, here are none but friends.

KITE. You know, sir, that you sent me to comfort the good woman in the straw, Mrs. Molly – my wife, Mr. Worthy.

WORTHY. Oho, very well – I wish you joy, Mr. Kite.

KITE. Your worship very well may – for I have got both a wife and a child in half an hour – but as I was a-saying, you sent me to comfort Mrs. Molly – my wife, I mean – but what d' ye think sir? She was better comforted before I came.

PLUME. As how?

KITE. Why, sir, a footman in a blue livery had brought her ten guineas to buy her baby clothes.

PLUME. Who, in the name of wonder, could send them?

KITE. Nay, sir, I must whisper that – (*Whispers* PLUME.) Mrs. Silvia.

PLUME. Silvia! Generous creature.

WORTHY. Silvia! Impossible.

KITE. Here be the guineas, sir; I took the gold as part of my wife's portion: nay, farther, sir, she sent word that the child should be taken all imaginable care of, and that she intended to stand god-mother. The same footman, as I was coming to you with this news, call'd after me, and told me that his lady would speak with me – I went; and upon hearing that you were come to town, she gave me half a guinea for the news, and order'd me to tell you, that Justice Balance, her father, who is just come out of the country, would be glad to see you.

PLUME. There's a girl for you, Worthy – is there anything of woman in this? No, 'tis noble and generous, manly friendship, show me another woman that would lose an inch of her prerogative that way, without tears, fits, and reproaches. The common jealousy of her sex, which is nothing but their avarice

of pleasure, she despises; and can part with the lover, though she
dies for the man – Come, Worthy, where's the best wine? For
there I'll quarter.

WORTHY. Horton has a fresh pipe of choice Barcelona, which
I would not let him pierce before, because I reserv'd the maidenhead of it for your welcome to town.

PLUME. Let's away then – Mr. Kite, wait on the lady with my
humble service, and tell her, that I shall only refresh a little, and
wait on her.

WORTHY. Hold, Kite – have you seen the other recruiting captain?

KITE. No, sir.

PLUME. Another, who is he?

WORTHY. My rival in the first place, and the most unaccountable
fellow – But I'll tell you more as we go.

Exeunt.

Act I, Scene ii

Scene, an apartment. MELINDA *and* SILVIA *meeting.*

MELINDA. Welcome to town, cousin Silvia. (*Salute.*) I envied you
your retreat in the country; for Shrewsbury, methinks, and all
your heads of shires, are the most irregular places for living; here
we have smoke, noise, scandal, affectation, and pretension; in
short, every thing to give the spleen, and nothing to divert it –
Then the air is intolerable.

SILVIA. Oh! Madam, I have heard the town commended for its air.

MELINDA. But you don't consider, Silvia, how long I have liv'd
in it! For I can assure you, that to a lady the least nice in her
constitution, no air can be good above half a year; change of air
I take to be the most agreeable of any variety in life.

SILVIA. As you say, cousin Melinda, there are several sorts of airs, airs in conversation, airs in behaviour, airs in dress; then we have our quality airs, our sickly airs, our reserved airs, and sometimes our impudent airs.

MELINDA. Pshaw – I talk only of the air we breathe, or more properly of that we taste – Have not you, Silvia, found a vast difference in the taste of airs?

SILVIA. Pray, cousin, are not vapours a sort of air? Taste air! You might as well tell me I may feed upon air; but prithee, my dear Melinda, don't put on such airs to me, your education and mine were just the same, and I remember the time when we never troubled our heads about air, but when the sharp air from the Welsh mountains made our noses drop in a cold morning at the boarding-school.

MELINDA. Our education, cousin, was the same, but our tempera-ments had nothing alike; you have the constitution of a horse –

SILVIA. So far as to be troubled with neither spleen, colic, nor vapours, I need no salt for my stomach, no hart's-horn for my head, nor wash for my complexion; I can gallop all the morning after the hunting horn, and all the evening after a fiddle: in short, I can do every thing with my father but drink and shoot flying; and I'm sure I can do every thing my mother could, were I put to the trial.

MELINDA. You're in a fair way of being put to 't; for I'm told, your Captain is come to town.

SILVIA. Ay, Melinda, he is come, and I'll take care he shan't go without a companion.

MELINDA. You're certainly mad, cousin.

SILVIA. *And there's a pleasure, sure, in being mad,*
Which none but madmen know.

MELINDA. Thou poor, romantic Quixote, hast thou the vanity to imagine that a young, sprightly officer that rambles o'er half the globe in half a year, can confine his thoughts to the little daughter of a country justice in an obscure corner of the world?

SILVIA. Pshaw! What care I for his thoughts? I should not like a man with confin'd thoughts, it shows a narrowness of soul. Constancy is but a dull, sleepy quality at best; they will hardly admit it among the manly virtues, nor do I think it deserves a place with bravery, knowledge, policy, justice, and some other qualities that are proper to that noble sex. In short, Melinda, I think a petticoat a mighty simple thing, and I'm heartily tir'd of my sex.

MELINDA. That is, you are tired of an appendix to our sex, that you can't so handsomely get rid of in petticoats as if you were in breeches – O' my conscience, Silvia, hadst thou been a man, thou hadst been the greatest rake in Christendom.

SILVIA. I should endeavour to know the world, which a man can never do thoroughly without half a hundred friendships, and as many amours. But now I think on 't, how stands your affair with Mr. Worthy?

MELINDA. He's my aversion.

SILVIA. Vapours!

MELINDA. What do you say, madam?

SILVIA. I say, that you should not use that honest fellow so inhumanely, he's a gentleman of parts and fortune, and beside that he's my Plume's friend; and by all that's sacred, if you don't use him better, I shall expect satisfaction.

MELINDA. Satisfaction! You begin to fancy yourself in breeches in good earnest – But to be plain with you, I like Worthy the worse for being so intimate with your captain; for I take him to be a loose, idle, unmannerly coxcomb.

SILVIA. Oh! Madam – you never saw him, perhaps, since you were mistress of twenty thousand pound; you only knew him when you were capitulating with Worthy for a settlement, which perhaps might encourage him to be a little loose and unmannerly with you.

MELINDA. What do you mean, madam?

SILVIA. My meaning needs no interpretation, madam.

MELINDA. Better it had, madam – for methinks you're too plain.

SILVIA. If you mean the plainness of my person, I think your lady-ship as plain as me to the full.

MELINDA. Were I assur'd of that, I should be glad to take up with a rake-helly officer as you do.

SILVIA. Again! Look 'ee, madam – you're in your own house.

MELINDA. And if you had kept in yours, I should have excus'd you.

SILVIA. Don't be troubled, madam – I shan't desire to have my visit return'd.

MELINDA. The sooner therefore you make an end of this, the better.

SILVIA. I'm easily advis'd to follow my inclinations – So, madam – your humble servant.

Exit.

MELINDA. Saucy thing!

Enter LUCY.

LUCY. What's the matter, madam?

MELINDA. Did you not see the proud nothing, how she swells upon the arrival of her fellow?

LUCY. Her fellow has not been long enough arriv'd to occasion any great swelling, madam – I don't believe she has seen him yet.

MELINDA. Nor shan't if I can help it; let me see – I have it – bring me pen and ink – hold, I'll go write in my closet.

LUCY. An answer to this letter, I hope, madam.

Presents a letter.

MELINDA. Who sent it?

LUCY. Your Captain, madam –

MELINDA. He's a fool, and I'm tired of him, send it back unopen'd.

LUCY. The messenger's gone, madam.

MELINDA. Then how shall I send an answer? Call him back immediately, while I go write.

Exeunt severally.

The end of the first act.

20

Act II, Scene i

Scene, an apartment. Enter JUSTICE BALANCE *and* PLUME.

BALANCE. Look 'ee, Captain, give us but blood for our money, and you shan't want men. I remember, that for some years of the last war, we had no blood nor wounds but in the officers' mouths, nothing for our millions but news papers not worth a reading, our armies did nothing but play at prison bars, and hide and seek with the enemy, but now ye have brought us colours, and standards, and prisoners; odsmylife, Captain, get us but another Mareschal of France, and I'll go my self for a soldier.

PLUME. Pray, Mr. Balance, how does your fair daughter?

BALANCE. Ah! Captain, what is my daughter to a Mareschal of France? We're upon a nobler subject, I want to have a particular description of the Battle of Hochstet.

PLUME. The battle, sir, was a very pretty battle as one should desire to see, but we were all so intent upon victory, that we never minded the battle; all that I know of the matter is, our general commanded us to beat the French, and we did so, and if he pleases to say the word, we'll do 't again – But pray, sir, how does Mrs. Silvia?

BALANCE. Still upon Silvia! For shame, Captain – you're engag'd already, wedded to the war, war is your mistress, and it is below a soldier to think of any other.

PLUME. As a mistress, I confess, but as a friend, Mr. Balance.

BALANCE. Come, come, Captain, never mince the matter, would not you debauch my daughter if you could?

PLUME. How sir! I hope she's not to be debauch'd.

BALANCE. Faith but she is, sir, and any woman in England of her age and complexion, by a man of your youth and vigour. Look 'ee, Captain, once I was young. and once an officer as you are; and I can guess at your thoughts now by what mine were then, and I remember very well, that I would have given one of my legs to have deluded the daughter of an old plain country gentleman, as like me as I was then like you.

PLUME. But, sir, was that country gentleman your friend and benefactor?

BALANCE. Not much of that.

PLUME There the comparison breaks; the favours, sir, that −

BALANCE. Pho! I hate speeches; if I have done you any service, Captain, 'twas to please my self, for I love thee, and if I could part with my girl, you should have her as soon as any young fellow I know; but I hope you have more honour than to quit the service, and she more prudence than to follow the camp: but she's at her own disposal, she has fifteen hundred pound in her pocket, and so, *(Calls.)* Silvia, Silvia!

Enter SILVIA.

SILVIA. There are some letters, sir, come by the post from London; I left them upon the table in your closet.

BALANCE. And here is a gentleman from Germany. *(Presents PLUME to her.)* Captain, you'll excuse me, I'll go read my letters, and wait on you.

Exit.

SILVIA. Sir, you're welcome to England.

PLUME. You are indebted to me a welcome, madam, since the hopes of receiving it from this fair hand was the principal cause of my seeing England.

SILVIA. I have often heard, that soldiers were sincere. Shall I venture to believe public report?

PLUME. You may, when 'tis back'd by private insurance; for I swear, madam, by the honour of my profession, that whatever dangers I went upon, it was with the hope of making my self more worthy of your esteem, and if I ever had thoughts of preserving my life, 'twas for the pleasure of dying at your feet.

SILVIA. Well, well, you shall die at my feet, or where you will; but you know, sir, there is a certain will and testament to be made before-hand.

PLUME. My will, madam, is made already, and there it is, (*Gives her a parchment.*) and if you please to open that parchment, which was drawn the evening before the Battle of Blenheim, you will find whom I left my heir.

SILVIA *opens the will and reads.*

SILVIA. 'Mrs. Silvia Balance' – Well, Captain, this is a handsome and a substantial compliment, but I can assure you I am much better pleas'd with the bare knowledge of your intention, than I should have been in the possession of your legacy; but methinks, sir, you should have left something to your little boy at the Castle.

PLUME (*aside*). That's home; my little boy! Lack-a-day, madam, that alone may convince you 'twas none of mine; why the girl, madam, is my sergeant's wife, and so the poor creature gave out that I was father, in hopes that my friends might support her in case of necessity; that was all, madam, – my boy! No, no.

Enter SERVANT.

SERVANT. Madam, my master has receiv'd some ill news from London, and desires to speak with you immediately, and he begs the Captain's pardon that he can't wait on him as he promis'd.

PLUME. Ill news! Heavens avert it; nothing could touch me nearer than to see that generous, worthy gentleman afflicted; I'll leave you to comfort him, and be assured that if my life and fortune can be any way serviceable to the father of my Silvia, she shall freely command both.

SILVIA. The necessity must be very pressing, that would engage me to do either.

Exeunt severally.

Act II, Scene ii

Scene changes to another apartment. Enter BALANCE *and* SILVIA.

SILVIA. Whilst there is life there is hope, sir; perhaps my brother may recover.

BALANCE. We have but little reason to expect it. Dr Kilman acquaints me here, that before this comes to my hands, he fears I shall have no son – Poor Owen! But the decree is just, I was pleas'd with the death of my father, because he left me an estate, and now I'm punish'd with the loss of an heir to inherit mine. I must now look upon you as the only hopes of my family, and I expect that the augmentation of your fortune will give you fresh thoughts and new prospects.

SILVIA. My desire of being punctual in my obedience, requires that you would be plain in your commands, sir.

BALANCE. The death of your brother makes you sole heiress to my estate, which three or four years hence will amount to twelve hundred pound per annum; this fortune gives you a fair claim to quality and a title; you must set a just value upon your self, and in plain terms, think no more of Captain Plume.

SILVIA. You have often commended the gentleman, sir.

BALANCE. And I do so still; he's a very pretty fellow; but though I lik'd him well enough for a bare son-in-law, I don't approve of him for an heir to my estate and family; fifteen hundred pound, indeed, I might trust in his hands, and it might do the young fellow a kindness, but odsmylife, twelve hundred pound a year would ruin him, quite turn his brain. A captain of foot worth twelve hundred pound a year! 'Tis a prodigy in nature: besides this, I have five or six thousand pounds in woods upon my estate; Oh, that would make him stark mad, for you must know that all captains have a mighty aversion to timber, they can't endure to see trees standing; then I should have some rogue of a builder by the help of his damn'd magic art transform my noble oaks and elms into cornishes, portals, sashes, birds, beasts, gods and devils, to adorn some maggoty, new-fashioned bauble upon the Thames; and then you should have a dog of a gardener bring a *habeas corpus* for my *terra firma*, remove it to Chelsea or Twitnam, and clap it into grass-plats and gravel-walks.

Enter a SERVANT.

SERVANT Sir, here's one below with a letter for your worship, but he will deliver it into no hands but your own.

BALANCE. Come, show me the messenger.

Exit with SERVANT.

SILVIA. Make the dispute between love and duty, and I am Prince Prettyman exactly – If my brother dies, ah! poor brother; if he lives, Ah! poor sister – 'Tis bad both ways; I'll try it again, follow my own inclinations and break my father's heart, or obey his commands and break my own; worse and worse – Suppose I take it thus – A moderate fortune, a pretty fellow and a pad, – or a fine estate, a coach and six, and an ass – That will never do neither.

Enter BALANCE *and* SERVANT.

BALANCE. Put four horses into the coach. (*To the* SERVANT, *who goes out.*) Silvia.

SILVIA. Sir.

BALANCE. How old were you when your mother died?

SILVIA. So young that I don't remember I ever had one; and you have been so careful, so indulgent to me since, that indeed I never wanted one.

BALANCE. Have I ever deny'd you any thing you asked of me?

SILVIA. Never, that I remember.

BALANCE. Then Silvia, I must beg that once in your life you would grant me a favour.

SILVIA. Why should you question it, sir?

BALANCE. I don't, but I would rather counsel than command – I don't propose this with the authority of a parent, but as the advice of your friend, that you would take the coach this moment and go into the country.

SILVIA. Does this advice, sir, proceed from the contents of the letter you receiv'd just now?

BALANCE. No matter; I shall be with you in three or four days, and then give you my reasons – But before you go, I expect you will make me one solemn promise.

SILVIA. Propose the thing, sir.

BALANCE. That you will never dispose of your self to any man, without my consent.

SILVIA. I promise.

BALANCE. Very well, and to be even with you, I promise that I will never dispose of you without your own consent; and so Silvia, the coach is ready; farewell. (*Leads her to the door and returns.*) Now she's gone, I'll examine the contents of this letter a little nearer.

(*Reads.*) *Sir, My intimacy with Mr. Worthy has drawn a secret from him that he had from his friend Captain Plume, and my friendship and relation to your family oblige me to give you timely notice of it; the Captain has dishonourable designs upon my cousin Silvia. Evils of this nature are more easily prevented than amended, and that you would immediately send my cousin into the country is the advice of,*

Sir, your humble servant,
Melinda.

Why, the devil's in the young fellows of this age, they're ten times worse than they were in my time; had he made my daughter a whore, and forswore it like a gentleman, I could have almost pardon'd it; but to tell tales before-hand is monstrous! Hang it, I can fetch down a woodcock or snipe, and why not a hat and feather? I have a case of good pistols, and have a good mind to try.

Enter WORTHY.

BALANCE. Worthy, your servant.

WORTHY. I'm sorry, sir, to be the messenger of ill news.

BALANCE. I apprehend it, sir; you have heard that my son Owen is past recovery –

WORTHY. My advices say he's dead, sir.

BALANCE. He's happy, and I am satisfied; the strokes of Heaven I can bear; but injuries from men, Mr. Worthy, are not so easily supported.

WORTHY. I hope, sir, you're under no apprehension of wrong from anybody?

BALANCE. You know I ought to be.

WORTHY. You wrong my honour, sir, in believing I could know any thing to your prejudice without resenting it as much as you should.

BALANCE. This letter, sir, which I tear in pieces to conceal the person that sent it, informs me that Plume has a design upon Silvia, and that you are privy to 't.

WORTHY. Nay then, sir, I must do myself justice and endeavour to find out the author. (*Takes up a piece of the letter.*) Sir, I know the hand, and if you refuse to discover the contents, Melinda shall tell me.

Going.

BALANCE. Hold, sir, the contents I have told you already, only with this circumstance, that her intimacy with Mr. Worthy had drawn the secret from him.

WORTHY. Her intimacy with me! – Dear sir, let me pick up the pieces of this letter, 'twill give me such a hank upon her pride, to have her own an intimacy under her hand, 'twas the luckiest accident. (*Gathering up the letter.*) The aspersion, sir, was nothing but malice, the effect of a little quarrel between her and Mrs. Silvia.

BALANCE. Are you sure of that, sir?

WORTHY. Her maid gave me the history of part of the battle just now, as she overheard it.

BALANCE. 'Tis probable, I am satisfied.

WORTHY. But I hope, sir, your daughter has suffer'd nothing upon the account?

BALANCE. No, no – Poor girl, she's so afflicted with the news of her brother's death, that to avoid company she beg'd leave to be gone into the country.

WORTHY. And is she gone?

BALANCE. I could not refuse her, she was so pressing, the coach went from the door the minute before you came –

WORTHY. So pressing to be gone, sir – I find her fortune will give her the same airs with Melinda, and then Plume and I may laugh at one another.

BALANCE. Like enough – Women are as subject to pride as we are, and why mayn't great women as well as great men forget their old acquaintance? – But come, where's this young fellow, I love him so well, it would break the heart of me to think him a rascal – (*Aside.*) I'm glad my daughter's gone fairly off tho'. – Where does the Captain quarter?

WORTHY. At Horton's, I'm to meet him there two hours hence, and we should be glad of your company.

BALANCE. Your pardon, dear Worthy, I must allow a day or two to the death of my son; the decorum of mourning is what we owe the world, because they pay it to us afterwards. I'm yours over a bottle, or how you will.

WORTHY. Sir, I'm your humble servant.

Exeunt severally.

Act II, Scene iii

Scene, the street. Enter KITE, *with one of the* MOB [PEARMAIN *and* APPLETREE] *in each hand, drunk.*

KITE (*sings*). *Our prentice Tom may now refuse*
    To wipe his scoundrel master's shoes;
    For now he's free to sing and play,
    Over the hills and far away – Over the hills, etc.

The MOB [APPLETREE *and* PEARMAIN] *sing the chorus.*

We all shall lead more happy lives,
By getting rid of brats and wives,
That scold and brawl both night and day;
Over the hills and far away – Over the hills, etc.

KITE. Hey, boys – Thus we soldiers live; drink, sing, dance, play;
we live, as one should say – We live – 'Tis impossible to tell how
we live – We're all princes – Why – Why, you're a king – You're
an emperor, and I'm a prince – Now – An't we –

APPLETREE. No, Sergeant I'll be no emperor.

KITE. No!

APPLETREE. No, I'll be a Justice of Peace.

KITE. A Justice of Peace, man!

APPLETREE. Aye, wauns will I, for since this Pressing Act they are
greater than any emperor under the sun.

KITE. Done; you're a Justice of Peace, and you're a king, and I'm a
duke, and a rum duke, an't I?

PEARMAIN. No, but I'll be no king.

KITE. What then?

PEARMAIN. I'll be a queen.

KITE. A queen!

PEARMAIN. Aye, Queen of England – That's greater than any
king of 'em all.

KITE. Bravely said! Faith: Huzza for the Queen!

All huzza.

But hark 'ee, you Mr. Justice and you Mr. Queen, did you ever
see the Queen's picture?

BOTH. No, no, no.

KITE. I wonder at that; I have two of 'em set in gold, and as like
Her Majesty, God bless the mark. (*He takes two broad pieces out of
his pocket.*) See here, they're set in gold.

Gives one to each.

APPLETREE (*looking earnestly upon the piece*). The wonderful works of nature!

PEARMAIN. What's this written about? Here's a posy, I believe, *Ca-ro-lus* – what's that, Sergeant?

KITE. Oh, Carolus – Why, Carolus is Latin for Queen Anne, that's all.

PEARMAIN. 'Tis a fine thing to be a scollard, Sergeant, will you part with this? I'll buy it on you, if it come within the compass of a crawn.

KITE. A crown! Never talk of buying – 'Tis the same thing among friends you know, I present them to you both, you shall give me as good a thing; put them up, and remember your old friend, when I'm (*Singing*) *over the hills and far away.*

They sing and put up the money. Enter PLUME *singing.*

PLUME. *Over the hills, and o'er the main,*
To Flanders, Portugal, or Spain;
The Queen commands, and we'll obey,
Over the hills and far away.

Come on my men of mirth, away with it, I'll make one among ye; who are these hearty lads?

KITE. Off with your hats, ouns, off with your hats; this is the Captain, the Captain.

APPLETREE. We have seen captains afore now, mun.

PEARMAIN. Aye, and lieutenant captains too; flesh, I'se keep on my nab.

APPLETREE. And I'se scarcely doff mine for any captain in England; my vether's a freeholder.

PLUME. Who are these jolly lads, Sergeant?

KITE. A couple of honest, brave fellows that are willing to serve the Queen; I have entertain'd 'em just now as volunteers under your honour's command.

PLUME. And good entertainment they shall have, volunteers are the men I want, those are the men fit to make soldiers, captains, generals.

PEARMAIN. Wauns, Tummas, what's this? Are you listed?

APPLETREE. Flesh, not I; are you, Costar?

PEARMAIN. Wauns, not I.

KITE. What, not listed! Ha, ha, ha, a very good jest, faith.

PEARMAIN. Come, Tummas, we'll go whome.

APPLETREE. Aye, aye, come.

KITE. Home! For shame, gentlemen, behave yourselves better before your Captain – dear Tummas, honest Costar –

PEARMAIN. No, no, we'll be gone. (*Going.*)

KITE. Nay, then I command you to stay: I place you both sentinels in this place for two hours to watch the motion of St Mary's clock, you, and you the motion of St Chad's; and he that dare stir from his post till he be relieved, shall have my sword in his guts the next minute.

PLUME. What's the matter, Sergeant – I'm afraid you're too rough with these gentlemen.

KITE. I'm too mild, sir, they disobey command, sir, and one of 'em should be shot for an example to the other.

PEARMAIN. Shot! Tummas.

PLUME. Come, gentlemen, what is the matter?

APPLETREE. We don't know; the noble Sergeant is pleased to be in a passion, sir – but –

KITE. They disobey command, they deny their being listed.

PEARMAIN. Nay, Sergeant, we don't downright deny it neither, that we dare not do for fear of being shot; but we humbly conceive in a civil way, and begging your worship's pardon, that we may go home.

PLUME. That's easily known; have either of you received any of the Queen's money?

APPLETREE. Not a brass farthing, sir.

KITE. Sir, they have each of 'em receiv'd three and twenty shillings and six-pence, and 'tis now in their pockets.

APPLETREE. Wauns! If I have a penny in my pocket but a bent six-pence, I'll be content to be listed, and shot into the bargain.

PEARMAIN. And I, look 'ee here, sir.

APPLETREE. Aye, here's my stock too, nothing but the Queen's picture that the Sergeant gave me just now.

KITE. See there, a broad piece, three and twenty shillings and sixpence; the t' other has the fellow on 't.

PLUME. The case is plain, gentlemen, the goods are found upon you: those pieces of gold are worth three and twenty and six-pence each.

PEARMAIN. So it seems that Carolus is three and twenty shillings and six-pence in Latin.

APPLETREE. 'Tis the same thing in the Greek, for we are listed.

PEARMAIN. Flesh, but we an't, Tummas, I desire to be carried before the mayor, Captain.

While they talk, the CAPTAIN *and* SERGEANT *whisper.*

PLUME. 'Twill never do, Kite; your damn'd tricks will ruin me at last, I won't lose the fellows tho', if I can help it – Well, gentlemen, there must be some trick in this, my Sergeant offers to take his oath that you're fairly listed.

APPLETREE. Why, Captain, we know that you soldiers have more liberty of conscience than other folks, but for me or neighbour Costar here to take such an oath, 'twould be downright perjuration.

PLUME. Look 'ee you rascal, you villain, if I find that you have impos'd upon these two honest fellows, I'll trample you to death, you dog! Come, how was 't?

APPLETREE. Nay, then we will speak, your Sergeant, as you say, is a rogue, begging your worship's pardon – And –

PEARMAIN. Nay, Tummas, let me speak, you know I can read? and so, sir, he gave us those two pieces of money for pictures of the Queen by way of a present.

PLUME. How! By way of a present! The son of a whore! I'll teach him to abuse honest fellows like you; Scoundrel, rogue, villain, *etc*.

Beats the SERGEANT *off the stage, and follows him out.*

BOTH. O brave, noble Captain, huzza, a brave Captain, faith.

PEARMAIN. Now, Tummas, Carolus is Latin for a beating: this is the bravest Captain I ever saw, wauns, I have a month's mind to go with him.

Re-enter PLUME.

PLUME. A dog! To abuse two such honest fellows as you; look 'ee, gentlemen, I love a pretty fellow, I come among you here as an officer to list soldiers, not as a kidnapper, to steal slaves.

PEARMAIN. Mind that, Tummas.

PLUME. I desire no man to go with me, but as I went myself: I went a volunteer, as you or you may go, for a little time carried a musket, and now I command a company.

APPLETREE. Mind that, Costar, a sweet gentleman.

PLUME. 'Tis true, gentlemen, I might take an advantage of you; the Queen's money was in your pockets; my Sergeant was ready to take his oath you were listed, but I scorn to do a base thing, you are both of you at your liberty.

PEARMAIN. Thank you, noble Captain. – I cod, I cannot find in my heart to leave him, he talks so finely.

APPLETREE. Ay, Costar, would he always hold in this mind.

PLUME. Come, my lads, one thing more I'll tell you, you're both young tight fellows, and the army is the place to make you men for ever: every man has his lot, and you have yours; what think you now of a purse full of French gold out of a monsieur's pocket, after you have dash'd out his brains with the butt of your firelock? eh! –

PEARMAIN. Wauns, I'll have it, Captain – give me a shilling, I'll follow you to the end of the world.

APPLETREE. Nay, dear Costar, duna, be advised.

PLUME. Here, my hero, here are two guineas for thee, as earnest of what I'll do farther for thee.

APPLETREE. Duna take it, duna, dear Costar.

Cries and pulls back his arm.

PEARMAIN I wull, I wull, wauns, my mind gives me that I shall be a captain myself; I take your money, sir, and now I'm a gentleman.

PLUME. Give me thy hand – And now you and I will travel the world o'er, and command wherever we tread – (*Aside.*) Bring your friend with you if you can.

PEARMAIN. Well, Tummas, must we part?

APPLETREE. No, Costar, I cannot leave thee. Come, Captain, (*Crying.*) I'll e'en go along too; and if you have two honester, simpler lads in your company than we twa been – I'll say no more –

PLUME. Here, my lad. (*Gives him money.*) Now your name?

APPLETREE. Thummas Appletree.

PLUME. And yours?

PEARMAIN. Costar Pearmain.

PLUME. Born where?

APPLETREE. Both in Herefordshire.

PLUME. Very well; courage, my lads, now we'll sing *Over the hills and far away.*

Courage, boys, 'tis one to ten,
But we return all gentlemen; etc.

Exeunt.

The end of the second act.

Act III, Scene i

Scene, the market-place. PLUME *and* WORTHY.

WORTHY. I can't forbear admiring the equality of our two fortunes: we lov'd two ladies; they met us half way, and just as we were upon the point of leaping into their arms, fortune drops into their laps, pride possesses their hearts, a maggot fills their heads, madness takes 'em by the tails, they snort, kick up their heels, and away they run.

PLUME. And leave us here to mourn upon the shore – a couple of poor, melancholy monsters – What shall we do?

WORTHY. I have a trick for mine; the letter you know, and the fortune-teller.

PLUME. And I have a trick for mine.

WORTHY. What is 't?

PLUME. I'll never think of her again.

WORTHY. No!

PLUME. No; I think my self above administering to the pride of any woman, were she worth twelve thousand a year, and I han't the vanity to believe I shall ever gain a lady worth twelve hundred; the generous, good-natured Silvia in her smock I admire, but the haughty, scornful Silvia, with her fortune, I despise.

A song.

1.

Come, fair one, be kind,
You never shall find
A fellow so fit for a lover:

The world shall view
My passion for you,
But never your passion discover.

2.

I still will complain
Of your frowns and disdain,
Tho' I revel thro' all your charms:
The world shall declare,
That I die with despair,
When I only die in your arms.

3.

I still will adore,
And love more and more,
But, by Jove, if you chance to prove cruel:
I'll get me a miss
That freely will kiss,
Tho' I afterwards drink water-gruel.

What, sneak out o' town, and not so much as a word, a line, a compliment! 'Sdeath, how far off does she live? I'll go and break her windows.

WORTHY. Ha, ha, ha; aye, and the window bars too to come at her. Come, come friend, no more of your rough military airs.

Enter KITE.

KITE. Captain, sir, look yonder, she's a-coming this way, 'tis the prettiest, cleanest, little tit –

PLUME. Now, Worthy, to show you how much I'm in love – Here she comes, and what is that great country fellow with her?

KITE. I can't tell, sir.

Enter ROSE *and her brother* BULLOCK, ROSE *with a basket on her arm, crying 'Chickens'.*

ROSE. Buy chickens, young and tender – young and tender chickens.

PLUME. Here, you chickens –

ROSE. Who calls?

PLUME. Come hither, pretty maid.

ROSE. Will you please to buy, sir?

WORTHY. Yes, child, we'll both buy.

PLUME. Nay, Worthy, that's not fair, market for yourself; come, child, I'll buy all you have.

ROSE. Then all I have is at your sarvice. (*Curtsies.*)

WORTHY. Then I must shift for myself, I find.

Exit.

PLUME. Let me see – young and tender, you say?

Chucks her under the chin.

ROSE. As ever you tasted in your life, sir. (*Curtsies.*)

PLUME. Come, I must examine your basket to the bottom, my dear.

ROSE. Nay, for that matter, put in your hand, feel, sir; I warrant my ware as good as any in the market.

PLUME. And I'll buy it all, child, were it ten times more.

ROSE. Sir, I can furnish you.

PLUME. Come then; we won't quarrel about the price, they're fine birds; pray what's your name, pretty creature?

ROSE. Rose, sir: my father is a farmer within three short mile o' th' town; we keep this market; I sell chickens, eggs, and butter, and my brother Bullock there sells corn.

BULLOCK. Come, sister, haste ye; we shall be liate a whome.

All this while BULLOCK *whistles about the stage.*

PLUME. Kite!

He tips the wink upon KITE, *who returns it.*

Pretty Mrs. Rose! You have – Let me see – How many?

ROSE. A dozen, sir – and they are richly worth a crawn.

BULLOCK. Come, Ruose, Ruose, I sold fifty stracke o' barley to day in half this time; but you will higgle and higgle for a penny more than the commodity is worth.

ROSE. What's that to you, oaf? I can make as much out of a groat as you can out of four-pence, I'm sure – The gentleman bids fair, and when I meet with a chapman, I know how to make the best on him – And so, sir, I say for a crawn piece the bargain's yours.

PLUME. Here's a guinea, my dear.

ROSE. I con't change your money, sir.

PLUME. Indeed, indeed but you can – My lodging is hard by, chickens, and we'll make change there.

Goes off, she follows him.

KITE. So, sir, as I was telling you, I have seen one of these hussars eat up a ravelin for his breakfast, and afterwards pick his teeth with a palisado.

BULLOCK. Aye, you soldiers see very strange things – But pray, sir, what is a ravelin?

KITE. Why 'tis like a modern minc'd pie, but the crust is confounded hard, and the plums are somewhat hard of digestion!

BULLOCK. Then your palisado, pray what may he be? – Come, Ruose, pray ha' done.

KITE. Your palisado is a pretty sort of bodkin, about the thickness of my leg.

BULLOCK (*aside*). – That's a fib, I believe. – Eh, where's Ruose? Ruose! Ruose! 'Sflesh, where's Ruose gone?

KITE. She's gone with the captain.

BULLOCK. The captain! Wauns, there's no pressing of women, sure?

KITE. But there is, sir.

BULLOCK. If the captain should press Ruose, I should be ruin'd; which way went she? – Oh! The devil take your rablins and palisadoes.

Exit.

KITE. You shall be better acquainted with them, honest Bullock, or I shall miss of my aim.

Enter WORTHY.

WORTHY. Why, thou'rt the most useful fellow in nature to your Captain, admirable in your way, I find.

KITE. Yes, sir, I understand my business, I will say it; you must know, sir, I was born a gypsy, and bred among that crew till I was ten year old, there I learn'd canting and lying; I was bought from my mother Cleopatra by a certain nobleman for three pistols, who liking my beauty made me his page; there I learn'd impudence and pimping; I was turn'd off for wearing my Lord's linen, and drinking my Lady's brandy, and then turn'd bailiff's follower, there I learn'd bullying and swearing – I at last got into the army, and there I learn'd whoring and drinking – so that if your worship pleases to cast up the whole sum, *viz.* canting, lying, impudence, pimping, bullying, swearing, whoring, drinking, and a halberd, you will find the sum total will amount to a recruiting sergeant.

WORTHY. And pray, what induc'd you to turn soldier?

KITE. Hunger and ambition – The fears of starving and hopes of a truncheon, led me along to a gentleman with a fair tongue and fair periwig, who loaded me with promises; but I gad 'twas the lightest load that I ever felt in my life – He promis'd to advance me, and indeed he did so – To a garret in the Savoy – I asked him why he put me in prison, he called me lying dog, and said I was in garrison, and indeed 'tis a garrison that may hold out till doom's-day before I should desire to take it again; but here comes Justice Balance.

Enter BALANCE *and* BULLOCK.

BALANCE. Here, you Sergeant, where's your Captain? Here's a poor foolish fellow comes clamouring to me with a complaint, that your Captain has press'd his sister; do you know anything of this matter, Worthy?

WORTHY. Ha, ha, ha, I know his sister is gone with Plume to his lodgings to sell him some chickens.

BALANCE. Is that all? The fellow's a fool.

BULLOCK. I know that, an't please you; but if your worship pleases to grant me a warrant to bring her before you for fear o' th' worst.

BALANCE. Thou art a mad fellow, thy sister's safe enough.

KITE (*aside*). I hope so too.

WORTHY. Hast thou no more sense, fellow, than to believe that the captain can list women?

BULLOCK. I know not whether they list them, or what they do with them, but I'm sure they carry as many women as men with them out of the country.

BALANCE. But how came you not to go along with your sister?

BULLOCK. Luord, sir, I thought no more of her going than I do of the day I shall die; but this gentleman here, not suspecting any hurt neither, I believe – You thought no harm, friend, did ye?

KITE. Lack-a-day, sir, not I. – (*Aside.*) Only that I believe I shall marry her tomorrow.

BALANCE. I begin to smell powder – Well, friend, but what did that gentleman with you?

BULLOCK. Why, sir, he entertain'd me with a fine story of a great fight between the Hungarians, I think it was, and the Irish. And so, sir, while we were in the heat of the battle, the Captain carried off the baggage.

BALANCE. Sergeant, go along with this fellow to your Captain, give him my humble service, and desire him to discharge the wench, tho' he has listed her.

BULLOCK. Ay – and if he ben't free for that, he shall have another man in her place.

KITE. Come, honest friend. – (*Aside.*) You shall go to my quarters instead of the Captain's.

Exeunt KITE *and* BULLOCK.

BALANCE. We must get this mad Captain his complement of men, and send him a-packing, else he'll over-run the country.

WORTHY. You see, sir, how little he values your daughter's disdain.

BALANCE. I like him the better; I was much such another fellow
at his age; I never set my heart upon any woman so much as
to make me uneasy at the disappointment, but what was very
surprising both to my self and friends, I chang'd o' th' sudden
from the most fickle lover to be the most constant husband in
the world; but how goes your affair with Melinda?

WORTHY. Very slowly, Cupid had formerly wings, but I think
in this age he goes upon crutches, or I fancy Venus had been
dallying with her cripple Vulcan when my amour commenc'd,
which has made it go on so lamely. My mistress has got a
Captain too, but such a Captain! As I live, yonder he comes.

BALANCE. Who? That bluff fellow in the sash. I don't know him.

WORTHY. But I engage he knows you, and every body at first sight;
his impudence were a prodigy, were not his ignorance propor-
tionable; he has the most universal acquaintance of any man
living, for he won't be alone, and nobody will keep him company
twice; then he's a Cæsar among the women, *veni, vidi, vici*, that's
all. If he has but talk'd with the maid, he swears he has lain with
the mistress; but the most surprising part of his character is his
memory, which is the most prodigious, and the most trifling in
the world.

BALANCE. I have met with such men, and I take this good-for-
nothing memory to proceed from a certain contexture of the
brain, which is purely adapted to impertinencies, and there they
lodge secure, the owner having no thoughts of his own to disturb
them. I have known a man as perfect as a chronologer as to the
day and year of most important transactions, but be altogether
ignorant of the causes, springs, or consequences of any one thing
of moment; I have known another acquire so much by travel, as
to tell you the names of most places in Europe, with their dis-
tances of miles, leagues, or hours, as punctually as a post-boy;
but for anything else, as ignorant as the horse that carries the
mail.

WORTHY. This is your man, sir, add but the traveller's privilege of
lying, and even that he abuses; this is the picture, behold the life!

Enter BRAZEN.

BRAZEN. Mr. Worthy, I'm your servant, and so forth – Hark 'ee my
dear –

WORTHY. Whispering, sir, before company is not manners, and
when no body's by, 'tis foolish.

BRAZEN. Company! *Mort de ma vie*, I beg the gentleman's pardon,
who is he?

WORTHY. Ask him.

BRAZEN. So I will – My dear, I'm your servant, and so forth, your
name, my dear?

BALANCE. Very laconic, sir.

BRAZEN. Laconick, a very good name truly; I have known several
of the Laconicks abroad. Poor Jack Laconick! He was killed at
the Battle of Landen. I remember that he had a blue ribband in
his hat that very day, and after he fell, we found a piece of neat's
tongue in his pocket.

BALANCE. Pray, sir, did the French attack us or we them at
Landen?

BRAZEN The French attack us! Oons, sir, are you a Jacobite?

BALANCE. Why that question?

BRAZEN Because none but a Jacobite could think that the French
durst attack us – No, sir, we attack'd them on the – I have reason
to remember the time, for I had two-and-twenty horses kill'd
under me that day.

WORTHY. Then, sir, you rid mighty hard.

BALANCE. Or perhaps, sir, like my countryman, you rid upon half
a dozen horses at once.

BRAZEN. What d'ye mean, gentlemen, I tell you they were kill'd;
all torn to pieces by cannon-shot, except six that I stak'd to death
upon the enemy's *chevaux de frise*.

BALANCE. Noble Captain, may I crave your name?

BRAZEN. Brazen, at your service.

BALANCE. Oh, Brazen! A very good name, I have known several of the Brazens abroad.

WORTHY. Do you know Captain Plume, sir?

BRAZEN Is he anything related to Frank Plume in Northampton-shire – Honest Frank! Many, many a dry bottle have we crack'd hand to fist; you must have known his brother Charles that was concern'd in the India Company, he married the daughter of old Tongue-Pad the Master in Chancery, a very pretty woman, only squinted a little, she died in childbed of her first child, but the child surviv'd, 'twas a daughter, but whether 'twas call'd Margaret or Marjory, upon my soul I can't remember – But, gentlemen, (*Looking on his watch.*) I must meet a lady, a twenty-thousand-pounder presently, upon the walk by the water – Worthy, your servant; Laconick, yours.

Exit.

BALANCE. If you can have so mean an opinion of Melinda, as to be jealous of this fellow, I think she ought to give you cause to be so.

WORTHY. I don't think she encourages him so much for gaining herself a lover, as to set me up a rival; were there any credit to be given to his words, I should believe Melinda had made him this assignation; I must go see – sir, you'll pardon me.

BALANCE. Aye, aye, sir, you're a man of business.

[*Exit* WORTHY.]

But what have we got here?

Enter ROSE *singing what she pleases.*

ROSE. And I shall be a lady, a Captain's lady, and ride single upon a white horse with a star, upon a velvet side-saddle, and I shall go to London and see the tombs and the lions, and the Queen. Sir – an't please your worship, I have often seen your worship ride thro' our grounds a-hunting, begging your worship's pardon – pray what may this lace be worth a yard?

Showing some lace.

BALANCE. Right Mechlin, by this light! Where did you get this lace, child?

ROSE. No matter for that, sir, I come honestly by 't.

BALANCE. I question it much.

ROSE. And see here, sir, a fine turkey-shell snuff-box, and fine mangeree, see here; *(She takes snuff affectedly.)* the Captain learnt me how to take it with an air.

BALANCE. Oho, the Captain! Now the murder's out, and so the Captain taught you to take it with an air?

ROSE. Yes, and give it with an air too – Will your worship please to taste my snuff?

Offers the box affectedly.

BALANCE. You're a very apt scholar, pretty maid, and pray what did you give the Captain for these fine things?

ROSE. He's to have my brother for a soldier, and two or three sweethearts that I have in the country, they shall all go with the Captain; oh, he's the finest man, and the humblest withal, would you believe it, sir? He carried me up with him to his own chamber with as much familiarity as if I had been the best lady in the land.

BALANCE. Oh he's a mighty familiar gentleman as can be.

ROSE. But I must beg your worship's pardon, I must go seek out my brother Bullock.

Runs off singing.

BALANCE. If all officers took the same method of recruiting with this gentleman, they might come in time to be fathers as well as captains of their companies.

Enter PLUME *singing.*

PLUME. *But it is not so*
With those that go
Thro' frost and snow
Most apropo,
My maid with the milking-pail.

Takes hold on ROSE

How, the Justice! Then I'm arraign'd, condemn'd, and executed.

BALANCE. Oh, my noble Captain.

ROSE. And my noble Captain too, sir.

PLUME. 'Sdeath, child, are you mad? – Mr. Balance, I am so full of business about my recruits, that I han't a moment's time to – I have just now three or four people to –

BALANCE. Nay, Captain, I must speak to you.

ROSE. And so must I too, Captain.

PLUME. Any other time, sir; I cannot for my life, sir –

BALANCE. Pray, sir.

PLUME. Twenty thousand things – I would but – now, sir, pray – devil take me I cannot – I must –

Breaks away.

BALANCE. Nay, I'll follow you.

Exit.

ROSE. And I too.

Exit.

Act III, Scene ii

Scene, the walk, by the Severn side. Enter MELINDA *and her maid* LUCY.

MELINDA. And pray, was it a ring, or buckle, or pendants, or knots; or in what shape was the almighty gold transform'd that has brib'd you so much in his favour?

LUCY. Indeed, madam, the last bribe I had was from the Captain, and that was only a small piece of Flanders edging for pinners.

MELINDA. Aye, Flanders lace, is as constant a present from officers to their women, as something else is from their women to them. They every year bring over a cargo of lace to cheat the Queen of her duty, and her subjects of their honesty.

LUCY. They only barter one sort of prohibited goods for another, madam.

MELINDA. Has any of them been bartering with you, Mrs. Pert, that you talk so like a trader?

LUCY. Madam, you talk as peevishly to me as if it were my fault; the crime is none of mine tho' I pretend to excuse it; tho' he should not see you this week, can I help it? But as I was saying, madam, his friend Captain Plume has so taken him up these two days –

MELINDA. Psha! would his friend, the Captain, were tied upon his back; I warrant he has never been sober since that confounded Captain came to town: the devil take all officers, I say, they do the nation more harm by debauching us at home, than they do good by defending us abroad: no sooner a captain comes to town, but all the young fellows flock about him, and we can't keep a man to ourselves.

LUCY. One would imagine, madam, by your concern for Worthy's absence, that you should use him better when he's with you.

MELINDA. Who told you, pray, that I was concern'd for his absence? I'm only vex'd that I've had nothing said to me these two days: one may like the love and despise the lover, I hope; as one may love the treason and hate the traitor. Oh! here comes another Captain, and a rogue that has the confidence to make love to me; but indeed I don't wonder at that, when he has the assurance to fancy himself a fine gentleman.

LUCY (*aside*). If he should speak o' th' assignation, I should be ruin'd.

Enter BRAZEN.

BRAZEN. True to the touch, faith. (*Aside.*) I'll draw up all my compliments into one grand platoon, and fire upon her at once.

Thou peerless princess of Salopian plains
Envied by nymphs and worshipp'd by the swains,
Behold how humbly do's the Severn glide,
To greet thee, princess of the Severn side.

Madam, I'm your humble servant and all that, madam – A fine river this same Severn, do you love fishing, madam?

MELINDA. 'Tis a pretty melancholy amusement for lovers.

BRAZEN. I'll go buy hooks and lines presently; for you must know, madam, that I have serv'd in Flanders against the French, in Hungary against the Turks, and in Tangier against the Moors, and I was never so much in love before; and split me, madam, in all the campaigns I ever made I have not seen so fine a woman as your ladyship.

MELINDA. And from all the men I ever saw I never had so fine a compliment; but you soldiers are the best-bred men, that we must allow.

BRAZEN. Some of us, madam, but there are brutes among us too, very sad brutes; for my own part, I have always had the good luck to prove agreeable: I have had very considerable offers, madam, I might have married a German princess worth fifty thousand crowns a year, but her stove disgusted me; the daughter of a Turkish bashaw fell in love with me too when I was prisoner among the infidels; she offer'd to rob her father of his treasure, and make her escape with me, but I don't know how, my time was not come; hanging and marriage, you know, go by destiny; fate has reserved me for a Shropshire lady with twenty thousand pound – Do you know any such person, madam?

MELINDA (*aside*). Extravagant coxcomb! – To be sure a great many ladies of that fortune would be proud of the name of Mrs. Brazen.

BRAZEN. Nay, for that matter, madam, there are women of very good quality of the name of Brazen.

Enter WORTHY.

MELINDA. Oh! are you there, gentleman? – Come, Captain, we'll walk this way, give me your hand.

BRAZEN. My hand, heart's blood and guts are at your service – Mr. Worthy, – your servant, my dear.

Exit leading MELINDA.

WORTHY. Death and fire! this is not to be borne.

Enter PLUME.

PLUME. No more it is, faith.

WORTHY. What?

PLUME. The March beer at the Raven; I have been doubly serving the Queen, – raising men and raising the Excise – recruiting and elections are rare friends to the Excise –

WORTHY. You an't drunk?

PLUME. No, no, whimsical only; I could be mighty foolish, and fancy myself mighty witty; reason still keeps its throne, but it nods a little, that's all.

WORTHY. Then you're just fit for a frolic?

PLUME. As fit as close pinners for a punk in the pit.

WORTHY. There's your play then, recover me that vessel from that Tangerine –

PLUME. She's well rigg'd, but how is she mann'd?

WORTHY. By Captain Brazen that I told you of today; the frigate is call'd the Melinda, a first rate I can assure you; she sheer'd off with him just now on purpose to affront me, but according to your advice I would take no notice, because I would seem to be above a concern for her behaviour; but have a care of a quarrel.

PLUME. No, no, I never quarrel with anything in my cups but with an oyster wench or a cook maid, and if they ben't civil, I knock 'em down; But hark 'ee my friend, I will make love, and I must make love, – I tell 'ee what, I'll make love like a platoon.

WORTHY. A platoon! how's that?

PLUME. I'll kneel, stoop and stand, faith; most ladies are gain'd by platooning.

WORTHY. Here they come; I must leave you.

Exit.

PLUME. So – now must I look as sober and demure as a whore at a christening.

Enter BRAZEN *and* MELINDA.

BRAZEN. Who's that, madam?

MELINDA. A brother officer of yours, I suppose, sir.

BRAZEN. Aye! (*To* PLUME.) My dear.

PLUME. My dear!

They run and embrace.

BRAZEN. My dear boy, how is 't? Your name, my dear? if I be not mistaken, I have seen your face.

PLUME. I never see yours in my life, my dear – but there's a face well known as the sun's, that shines on all, and is by all adored.

BRAZEN. Have you any pretensions, sir?

PLUME. Pretensions!

BRAZEN. That is, sir, have you ever serv'd abroad?

PLUME. I have serv'd at home, sir; for ages serv'd this cruel fair –
And that will serve the turn, sir.

MELINDA (*aside*). So – between the fool and the rake I shall bring a fine spot of work upon my hands – I see Worthy yonder, I could be content to be friends with him would he come this way.

BRAZEN. Will you fight for the lady, sir?

PLUME. No, sir, but I'll have her notwithstanding.

Thou peerless princess of Salopian plains,
Envied by nymphs and worshipp'd by the swains.

BRAZEN. Oons, sir, not fight for her!

PLUME. Prithee be quiet, I shall be out.

Behold how humbly do's the Severn glide
To greet thee, princess of the Severn side.

BRAZEN. Don't mind him, madam, if he were not so well dressed I should take him for a poet; but I'll show the difference presently – Come, madam, we'll place you between us, and now the longest sword carries her.

Draws, MELINDA *shrieks. Enter* WORTHY.

MELINDA. Oh! Mr. Worthy, save me from these madmen.

Runs off with WORTHY.

PLUME. Ha, ha, ha, why don't you follow, sir, and fight the bold ravisher?

BRAZEN. No, sir, you're my man.

PLUME. I don't like the wages, and I won't be your man.

BRAZEN. Then you're not worth my sword.

PLUME. No! Pray what did it cost?

BRAZEN. It cost my enemies thousands of lives, sir.

PLUME. Then they had a dear bargain.

Enter SILVIA *dressed in man's apparel.*

SILVIA. Save ye, save ye, gentlemen.

BRAZEN. My dear, I'm yours.

PLUME. Do you know the gentleman?

BRAZEN. No, but I will presently – Your name, my dear?

SILVIA. Wilful, Jack Wilful, at your service.

BRAZEN. What! The Kentish Wilfuls, or those of Staffordshire?

SILVIA. Both, sir, both; I'm related to all the Wilfuls in Europe, and I'm head of the family at present.

PLUME. Do you live in this country, sir?

SILVIA. Yes, sir, I live where I stand, I have neither home, house, nor habitation beyond this spot of ground.

BRAZEN. What are you, sir?

SILVIA. A rake.

PLUME. In the army, I presume.

SILVIA. No, but intend to list immediately – Look 'ee, gentlemen, he that bids me fairest has me.

BRAZEN. Sir, I'll prefer you, I'll make you a corporal this minute.

PLUME. A corporal! I'll make you my companion, you shall eat with me.

BRAZEN. You shall drink with me.

PLUME. You shall lie with me, you young rogue. (*Kisses her.*)

BRAZEN. You shall receive your pay, and do no duty.

SILVIA. Then you must make me a field-officer.

PLUME. Pho, pho, I'll do more than all this, I'll make you a corporal, and give you a brevet for sergeant.

BRAZEN. Can you read and write, sir?

SILVIA. Yes.

BRAZEN. Then your business is done, I'll make you chaplain to the regiment.

SILVIA. Your promises are so equal that I'm at a loss to choose, there is one Plume that I hear much commended in town, pray which of you is Captain Plume?

PLUME. I am Captain Plume.

BRAZEN. No, no, I'm Captain Plume.

SILVIA. Hey day!

PLUME. Captain Plume, I'm your servant, my dear.

BRAZEN. Captain Brazen, I'm yours – The fellow dare not fight.

Enter KITE, *goes to whisper* PLUME.

KITE. Sir, if you please –

PLUME. No, no, there's your captain – Captain Plume, your sergeant here has got so drunk he mistakes me for you.

BRAZEN. He's an incorrigible sot – Here, my Hector of Holborn, forty shillings for you.

PLUME. I forbid the banns – Look 'ee, friend, you shall list with Captain Brazen.

SILVIA. I will see Captain Brazen hang'd first, I will list with Captain Plume; I'm a free-born Englishman and will be a slave my own way – (*To* BRAZEN.) Look 'ee, sir, will you stand by me?

BRAZEN. I warrant you, my lad.

SILVIA. Then I will tell you, Captain Brazen, (*To* PLUME.) that you are an ignorant, pretending, impudent coxcomb.

BRAZEN. Aye, aye, a sad dog.

SILVIA. A very sad dog, give me the money noble Captain Plume.

PLUME. Hold, hold, then you won't list with Captain Brazen?

SILVIA. I won't.

BRAZEN. Never mind him, child, I'll end the dispute presently; hark 'ee, my dear.

Takes PLUME *to one side of the stage, and entertains him in dumb show.*

KITE. Sir, he in the plain coat is Captain Plume, I'm his Sergeant, and will take my oath on 't.

SILVIA. What! Are you Sergeant Kite?

KITE. At your service.

SILVIA. Then I would not take your oath for a farthing.

KITE. A very understanding youth of his age! Pray sir, let me look you full in the face.

SILVIA. Well, sir, what have you to say to my face?

KITE. The very image and superscription of my brother, two bullets of the same calibre were never so like; sure it must be Charles, Charles –

SILVIA. What d' ye mean by Charles?

KITE. The voice too, only a little variation in *effa ut flat;* my dear brother, for I must call you so, if you should have the fortune to enter into the most noble society of the sword, I bespeak you for a comrade.

SILVIA. No, sir, I'll be your Captain's comrade if any body's.

KITE. Ambition! There again, 'tis a noble passion for a soldier; by that I gain'd this glorious halberd. Ambition! I see a commission in his face already, pray noble Captain give me leave to salute you.

Offers to kiss her.

SILVIA. What, men kiss one another!

KITE. We officers do, 'tis our way; we live together like man and wife, always either kissing or fighting – But I see a storm a-coming.

SILVIA. Now, Sergeant, I shall see who is your Captain by your knocking down the t' other.

KITE. My captain scorns assistance, sir.

BRAZEN. How dare you contend for any thing, and not dare to draw your sword? But you're a young fellow, and have not been much abroad, I excuse that; but prithee resign the man, prithee do, you're a very honest fellow.

PLUME. You lie, and you're a son of a whore.

Draws, and makes up to BRAZEN.

BRAZEN (*retiring*). Hold, hold, did not you refuse to fight for the lady?

PLUME. I always do, but for a man I'll fight knee deep, so you lie again.

   PLUME *and* BRAZEN *fight a traverse or two about the stage;* SILVIA *draws, and is held by* KITE, *who sounds to arms with his mouth, takes* SILVIA *in his arms, and carries her off the stage.*

BRAZEN. Hold – where's the man?

PLUME. Gone.

BRAZEN Then what do we fight for? (*Puts up.*) Now let's embrace, my dear.

PLUME. With all my heart, my dear. (*Putting up.*) I suppose Kite has listed him by this time.

They embrace.

BRAZEN You're a brave fellow. I always fight with a man before I make him my friend; and if once I find he will fight, I never quarrel with him afterwards – And now I'll tell you a secret, my dear friend, that lady we frighted out o 'the walk just now I found in bed this morning, so beautiful, so inviting – I presently lock'd the door – But I'm a man of honour – But I believe I shall marry her nevertheless; her twenty thousand pound you know will be a pretty convenience. I had an assignation with her here, but your coming spoil'd my sport, curse ye, my dear, – but don't do so again.

PLUME. No, no, my dear, men are my business at present.

Exeunt.

The end of the third act.

Act IV, Scene i

Scene of the walk continues. ROSE *and* BULLOCK *meeting.*

ROSE. Where have you been, you great booby, you're always out
o' th' way in the time of preferment?

BULLOCK. Preferment! who should prefer me?

ROSE. I would prefer you, who should prefer a man but a woman?
Come throw away that great club, hold up your head, cock your
hat, and look big.

BULLOCK. Ah! Ruose, Ruose, I fear somebody will look big sooner
than folk think of; this genteel breeding never comes into the
country without a train of followers. – Here has been Cartwheel
your sweet-heart, what will become o' him?

ROSE. Look 'ee, I'm a great woman and will provide for my
relations; I told the Captain how finely he could play upon the
tabor and pipe, so he has set him down for a drum-major.

BULLOCK. Nay, sister, why did not you keep that place for me?
You know I always lov'd to be a-drumming, if it were but on a
table, or on a quart pot.

Enter SILVIA.

SILVIA. Had I but a commission in my pocket I fancy my breeches
would become me as well as any ranting fellow of 'um all; for I
take a bold step, a rakish toss, a smart cock, and an impudent air
to be the principal ingredients in the composition of a captain. –
What's here? Rose, my nurse's daughter! I'll go and practise –
Come, child, kiss me at once. (*Kisses* ROSE.) And her brother
too! – Well, honest Dungfork, do you know the difference
between a horse cart and a cart horse, eh?

BULLOCK. I presume that your worship is a captain by your clothes and your courage.

SILVIA. Suppose I were, would you be contented to list, friend?

ROSE. No, no, tho' your worship be a handsome man, there be others as fine as you; my brother is engag'd to Captain Plume.

SILVIA. Plume! Do you know Captain Plume?

ROSE. Yes, I do, and he knows me. – He took the very ribbands out of his shirt sleeves and put 'em into my shoes. – See there – I can assure you that I can do any thing with the Captain.

BULLOCK. That is, in a modest way, sir. – Have a care what you say, Ruose, don't shame your parentage.

ROSE. Nay, for that matter I am not so simple as to say that I can do any thing with the Captain, but what I may do with any body else.

SILVIA. Soh! – and pray what do you expect from this Captain, child?

ROSE. I expect, sir! I expect, – but he order'd me to tell nobody – but suppose that he should promise to marry me?

SILVIA. You should have a care, my dear, men will promise any thing before-hand.

ROSE. I know that, but he promis'd to marry me afterwards.

BULLOCK. Wauns, Ruose, what have you said?

SILVIA. Afterwards! after what?

ROSE. After I had sold him my chickens. – I hope there's no harm in that, tho' there be an ugly song of chickens and sparagus.

Enter PLUME.

PLUME. What, Mr. Wilful, so close with my market woman!

SILVIA (*aside*). I'll try if he loves her. – Close, sir! aye, and closer yet, sir – Come, my pretty maid, you and I will withdraw a little.

PLUME. No, no, friend, I han't done with her yet.

SILVIA. Nor have I begun with her, so I have as good a right as you have.

PLUME. Thou art a bloody impudent fellow.

SILVIA. Sir, I would qualify myself for the service.

PLUME. Hast thou really a mind to the service?

SILVIA. Yes, sir: so let her go.

ROSE. Pray, gentlemen, don't be so violent.

PLUME. Come, leave it to the girl's own choice – will you belong to me or to that gentleman?

ROSE. Let me consider, you're both very handsome.

PLUME (*aside*). Now the natural inconstancy of her sex begins to work.

ROSE. Pray sir, what will you give me?

BULLOCK. Don't be angry, sir, that my sister should be mercenary, for she's but young.

SILVIA. Give thee, child! – I'll set thee above scandal; you shall have a coach with six before and six behind; an equipage to make vice fashionable, and put virtue out of countenance.

PLUME. Pho, that's easily done; I'll do more for thee, child, I'll buy you a furbelow scarf, and give you a ticket to see a play.

BULLOCK. A play! Wauns, Ruose, take the ticket, and let's see the show.

SILVIA. Look 'ee, Captain, if you won't resign, I'll go list with Captain Brazen this minute.

PLUME. Will you list with me if I give up my title?

SILVIA. I will.

PLUME. Take her – I'll change a woman for a man at any time.

ROSE. I have heard before indeed that you captains used to sell your men. (*Cries.*)

BULLOCK (*crying*). Pray, Captain, don't send Ruose to the West Indies.

PLUME. Ha, ha, ha, West Indies! no, no, my honest lad, give me thy hand; nor you nor she shall move a step farther than I do. – This gentleman is one of us, and will be kind to you, Mrs. Rose.

ROSE. But will you be so kind to me, sir, as the Captain would?

SILVIA. I can't be altogether so kind to you, my circumstances are not so good as the Captain's – but I'll take care of you, upon my word.

PLUME. Aye, aye, we'll all take care of her, – she shall live like a princess, and her brother here shall he – what would you be?

BULLOCK. Ah! sir, if you had not promis'd the place of drum-major –

PLUME. Aye, that is promis'd – but what think ye of barrack-master? You're a person of understanding, and barrack-master you shall be. – But what's become of this same Cartwheel you told me of, my dear?

ROSE. We'll go fetch him – come, brother barrack-master – we shall find you at home, noble Captain?

Exeunt ROSE *and* BULLOCK.

PLUME. Yes, yes – and now, sir, here are your forty shillings.

SILVIA. Captain Plume, I despise your listing-money; if I do serve, 'tis purely for love – of that wench I mean; for you must know, that among my other sallies, I have spent the best part of my fortune in search of a maid, and could never find one hitherto; so you may be assur'd I'd not sell my freedom under a less purchase than I did my estate, – so before I list I must be certified that this girl is a virgin.

PLUME Mr. Wilful, I can't tell how you can be certified in that point, till you try, but upon my honour she may be a vestal for ought that I know to the contrary. – I gain'd her heart indeed by some trifling presents and promises, and knowing that the best security for a woman's soul is her body, I would have made my self master of that too, had not the jealousy of my impertinent landlady interpos'd.

SILVIA. So you only want an opportunity for accomplishing your designs upon her?

PLUME. Not at all, I have already gain'd my ends, which were only the drawing in one or two of her followers; the women, you know, are the lodestones every where – gain the wives, and you're caressed by the husbands; please the mistresses and you are valu'd by their gallants; secure an interest with the finest women at court, and you procure the favour of the greatest men: so kiss the prettiest country wenches, and you are sure of listing the lustiest fellows. Some people may call this artifice, but I term it stratagem, since it is so main a part of the service – Besides, the fatigue of recruiting is so intolerable, that unless we could make ourselves some pleasure amidst the pain, no mortal man would be able to bear it.

SILVIA. Well, sir, I'm satisfied as to the point in debate – but now let me beg you to lay aside your recruiting airs, put on the man of honour, and tell me plainly what usage I must expect when I'm under your command.

PLUME. You must know in the first place then, that I hate to have gentlemen in my company, for they are always troublesome and expensive, sometimes dangerous; and 'tis a constant maxim amongst us, that those who know the least obey the best. Notwithstanding all this, I find something so agreeable about you, that engages me to court your company; and I can't tell how it is, but I should be uneasy to see you under the command of any body else. Your usage will chiefly depend upon your behaviour, only this you must expect, that if you commit a small fault I will excuse it, if a great one, I'll discharge you, for something tells me I shall not be able to punish you.

SILVIA. And something tells me, that if you do discharge me 'twill be the greatest punishment you can inflict; for were we this moment to go upon the greatest dangers in your profession, they would be less terrible to me than to stay behind you. – And now your hand, – this lists me – and now you are my Captain.

PLUME. Your friend – (*Kisses her.*) 'Sdeath! There's something in this fellow that charms me.

SILVIA. One favour I must beg – This affair will make some noise, and I have some friends that would censure my conduct if I threw myself into the circumstance of a private sentinel of my own head, I must therefore take care to be impress'd by the Act of Parliament, you shall leave that to me.

PLUME. What you please as to that – Will you lodge at my quarters in the mean time? You shall have part of my bed.

SILVIA. Oh, fie, lie with a common soldier! – would not you rather lie with a common woman?

PLUME. No, faith, I am not that rake that the world imagines; I have got an air of freedom, which people mistake for lewdness in me, as they mistake formality in others for religion; the world is all a cheat, only I take mine which is undesign'd to be more excusable than theirs, which is hypocritical; I hurt nobody but my self, and they abuse all mankind. – Will you lie with me?

SILVIA. No, no, Captain, you forget Rose, she's to be my bed-fellow you know.

PLUME. I had forgot, pray be kind to her.

Exeunt severally. Enter MELINDA *and* LUCY.

MELINDA. 'Tis the greatest misfortune in nature for a woman to want a confidante, we are so weak that we can do nothing without assistance, and then a secret racks us worse than the colic; I'm at this minute so sick of a secret, that I'm ready to faint away – help me, Lucy.

LUCY. Bless me, madam, what's the matter?

MELINDA. Vapours only – I begin to recover – if Silvia were in town, I could heartily forgive her faults for the ease of discovering my own.

LUCY. You're thoughtful, madam; am not I worthy to know the cause?

MELINDA. You're a servant, and a secret would make you saucy.

LUCY. Not unless you should find fault without a cause, madam.

MELINDA. Cause or not cause, I must not lose the pleasure of chiding when I please; women must discharge their vapours some where, and before we get husbands, our servants must expect to bear with 'em.

LUCY. Then, madam, you had better raise me to a degree above a servant: you know my family, and that five hundred pound would set me upon the foot of a gentlewoman, and make me worthy the confidence of any lady in the land; besides, madam, 'twill extremely encourage me in the great design I now have in hand.

MELINDA. I don't find that your design can be of any great advantage to you: 'twill please me indeed in the humour I have of being reveng'd on the fool for his vanity of making love to me, so I don't much care if I do promise you five hundred pound the day of my marriage.

LUCY. That is the way, madam, to make me diligent in the vocation of a confidante, which I think is generally to bring people together.

MELINDA. Oh, Lucy, I can hold my secret no longer – you must know that hearing of the famous fortune-teller in town, I went disguis'd to satisfy a curiosity which has cost me dear; that fellow is certainly the devil, or one of his bosom-favourites, he has told me the most surprising things of my past life –

LUCY. Things past, madam, can hardly be reckon'd surprising, because we know them already; did he tell you anything surprising that was to come?

MELINDA. One thing very surprising, he said I should die a maid.

LUCY. Die a maid– Come into the world for nothing! Dear madam, if you should believe him, it might come to pass; for the bare thought on 't might kill one in four and twenty hours – And did you ask him any questions about me?

MELINDA. You! Why, I pass'd for you.

LUCY. So 'tis I that am to die a maid – but the devil was a liar from the beginning, he can't make me die a maid – I have put it out of his power already.

MELINDA. I do but jest, I would have pass'd for you, and call'd my self Lucy, but he presently told me my name, my quality, my

fortune, and gave me the whole history of my life; he told me of
a lover I had in this country, and describ'd Worthy exactly, but in
nothing so well as in his present indifference – I fled to him for
refuge here to day – he never so much as encouraged me in
my fright, but coldly told me that he was sorry for the accident,
because it might give the town cause to censure my conduct;
excus'd his not waiting on me home, made me a careless bow,
and walked off. 'Sdeath, I could have stabb'd him, or my self,
'twas the same thing – Yonder he comes – I will so slave him.

LUCY. Don't exasperate him, consider what the fortune-teller told
you; men are scarce, and as times go, it is not impossible for a
woman to die a maid.

Enter WORTHY.

MELINDA. No matter.

WORTHY. I find she's warm'd, I must strike while the iron is hot, –
You have a great deal of courage, madam, to venture into the
walks where you were so late frighted.

MELINDA. And you have a quantity of impudence to appear
before me, that you have so lately affronted.

WORTHY. I had no design to affront you, nor appear before you
either, madam; I left you here because I had business in another
place, and came hither thinking to meet another person.

MELINDA. Since you find your self disappointed, I hope you'll
withdraw to another part of the walk.

WORTHY. The walk is as free for me as you, madam, and broad
enough for us both.

*They walk by one another, he with his hat cocked, she fretting and tearing her
fan.*

Will you please to take snuff, madam?

*He offers her his box, she strikes it out of his hand; while he is gathering
it up, enter* BRAZEN, *who takes* MELINDA *about the middle, she
cuffs him.*

BRAZEN What, here before me! My dear!

MELINDA. What means this insolence?

LUCY (*runs to* BRAZEN). Are you mad? Don't you see Mr. Worthy?

BRAZEN No, no, I'm struck blind – Worthy! Adso, well turn'd, my mistress has wit at her fingers' ends – madam, I ask your pardon, 'tis our way abroad – Mr. Worthy, you're the happy man.

WORTHY. I don't envy your happiness very much, if the lady can afford no other sort of favours but what she has bestow'd upon you.

MELINDA. I'm sorry the favour miscarried, for it was design'd for you, Mr. Worthy; and be assur'd, 'tis the last and only favour you must expect at my hands – Captain, I ask your pardon.

Exit with LUCY.

BRAZEN. I grant it – You see, Mr. Worthy, 'twas only a random shot, it might ha' taken off your head as well as mine – courage, my dear, 'tis the fortune of war – but the enemy has thought fit to withdraw, I think.

WORTHY. Withdraw! Oons, sir, what d' ye mean by withdraw?

BRAZEN. I'll show you.

Exit.

WORTHY. She's lost, irrecoverably lost, and Plume's advice has ruin'd me; 'sdeath, why should I that knew her haughty spirit be rul'd by a man that's a stranger to her pride.

Enter PLUME.

PLUME. Ha, ha, ha, a battle royal; don't frown so, man, she's your own, I tell 'ee; I saw the fury of her love in the extremity of her passion: the wildness of her anger is a certain sign that she loves you to madness; that rogue, Kite, began the battle with abundance of conduct, and will bring you off victorious, my life on 't; he plays his part admirably, she's to be with him again presently.

WORTHY. But what could be the meaning of Brazen's familiarity with her?

PLUME. You are no logician if you pretend to draw consequences from the actions of fools, there's no arguing by the rule of reason upon a science without principles, and such is their conduct; whim, unaccountable whim, hurries them on, like a man drunk with brandy before ten o'clock in the morning – But we lose our sport, Kite has open'd above an hour ago, let's away.

Exeunt.

Act IV, Scene ii

Scene: a chamber; a table with books and globes. KITE, *disguis'd in a strange habit, and sitting at the table.*

KITE (*rising*). By the position of the heavens, gain'd from my observation upon these celestial globes, I find that Luna was a tide-waiter, Sol a surveyor, Mercury a thief, Venus a whore, Saturn an alderman, Jupiter a rake, and Mars a Sergeant of Grenadiers – and this is the system of Kite the conjurer.

Enter PLUME *and* WORTHY.

PLUME. Well, what success?

KITE. I have sent away a shoemaker and a tailor already, one's to be a captain or marines and the other a major of dragoons, I am to manage them at night – Have you seen the lady, Mr. Worthy?

WORTHY. Aye, but it won't do – have you show'd her her name that I tore off from the bottom of the letter?

KITE. No, sir, I reserve that for the last stroke.

PLUME. What letter?

WORTHY. One that I would not let you see, for fear you should break Melinda's windows in good earnest.

Knocking at the door.

KITE. Officers to your post –

Exeunt WORTHY *and* PLUME.

Tycho, mind the door.

SERVANT *opens the door, enter a* SMITH.

SMITH. Well, master, are you the cunning man?

KITE. I am the learn'd Copernicus.

SMITH. Well, Master Coppernose, I'm but a poor man, and I can't. afford above a shilling for my fortune.

KITE. Perhaps, that is more than 'tis worth.

SMITH. Look 'ee, doctor, let me have something that's good for my shilling, or I'll have my money again.

KITE. If there be faith in the stars, you shall have your shilling forty fold. Your hand, countryman – You are by trade a smith.

SMITH How the devil should you know that?

KITE. Because the devil and you are brother tradesmen – You were born under Forceps.

SMITH. Forceps! What's that?

KITE. One of the signs; there's Leo, Sagittarius, Forceps, Furns, Dixmude, Namur, Brussels, Charleroy, and so forth – Twelve of 'em – Let me see – Did you ever make any bombs or cannon bullets?

SMITH. Not I.

KITE. You either have, or will – the stars have decreed that you shall be – I must have more money, sir, your fortune's great –

SMITH. Faith, doctor, I have no more.

KITE. Oh, sir, I'll trust you, and take it out of your arrears.

SMITH. Arrears! What arrears?

KITE. The five hundred pound that's owing to you from the government.

SMITH. Owing me!

KITE. Owing you, sir – let me see your t' other hand – I beg your pardon, it will be owing to you; and the rogue of an agent will demand fifty per cent for a fortnight's advance.

SMITH. I'm in the clouds, doctor, all this while.

KITE. So am I, sir, among the stars – In two years, three months, and two hours, you will be made Captain of the Forges to the grand Train of Artillery, and will have ten shillings a day and two servants; 'tis the decree of the stars and of the fix'd stars, that are as immovable as your anvil – Strike, sir, while the iron is hot – Fly, sir, begone –

SMITH. What, what would you have me do, doctor? I wish the stars would put me in a way for this fine place.

KITE. The stars do – let me see – aye, about an hour hence walk carelessly into the market-place, and you'll see a tall, slender gentleman cheapening a pen'worth of apples, with a cane hanging upon his button – This gentleman will ask you – what's o'clock – he's your man, and the maker of your fortune; follow him, follow him: and now go home, and take leave of your wife and children – an hour hence exactly is your time.

SMITH. A tall, slender gentleman, you say! With a cane, pray, what sort of a head has the cane?

KITE. An amber head, with a black ribband.

SMITH. But pray, of what employment is the gentleman?

KITE. Let me see – he's either a collector of the Excise, a pleni-potentiary, or a captain of grenadiers – I can't tell exactly which – but he'll call you honest – your name is –

SMITH. Thomas.

KITE. Right, he'll call you honest Tom –

SMITH. But how the devil should he know my name?

KITE. Oh, there are several sorts of Toms – Tom a Lincoln, Tom-tit, Tom Telltroth, Tom o' Bedlam, Tom Fool. –

Knocking at the door.

Be gone – an hour hence precisely –

SMITH. You say he'll ask me what's o'clock?

KITE. Most certainly, and you'll answer – you don't know, and be sure you look at St Mary's dial, for the sun won't shine, and if it should, you won't be able to tell the figures.

SMITH. I will, I will.

Exit.

PLUME (*behind*). Well done, conjurer, go on and prosper.

KITE. As you were.

Enter a BUTCHER

KITE (*aside*). What, my old friend Pluck, the butcher – I offer'd the surly bull-dog five guineas this morning, and he refused it.

BUTCHER. So, Master Conjurer – here's half a crown – and now you must understand –

KITE. Hold, friend, I know your business beforehand.

BUTCHER. You're devilish cunning then; for I don't well know it my self.

KITE. I know more than you, friend – You have a foolish saying, that such a one knows no more than the man-in-the-moon; I tell you the man-in-the-moon knows more than all the men under the sun: don't the moon see all the world?

BUTCHER. All the world see the moon, I must confess.

KITE. Then she must see all the world, that's certain – Give me your hand – you are by trade either a butcher or a surgeon.

BUTCHER. True – I am a butcher.

KITE. And a surgeon you will be, the employments differ only in the name – he that can cut up an ox, may dissect a man; and the same dexterity that cracks a marrow-bone, will cut off a leg or an arm.

BUTCHER. What d' ye mean, doctor, what d' ye mean?

KITE. Patience, patience, Mr. Surgeon General, the stars are great bodies, and move slowly.

BUTCHER. But what d' ye mean by Surgeon General, doctor?

KITE. Nay, sir, if your worship won't have patience, I must beg the favour of your worship's absence.

BUTCHER. My worship, my worship! But why my worship?

KITE. Nay, then I have done.

Sits.

BUTCHER. Pray, doctor.

KITE. Fire and fury, sir! (*Rises in a passion.*) Do you think the stars will be hurried – Do the stars owe you any money, sir, that you dare to dun their lordships at this rate – Sir, I am porter to the stars, and I am order'd to let no dun come near their doors.

BUTCHER. Dear doctor, I never had any dealings with the stars, they don't owe me a penny – But since you are the porter, please to accept of this half crown to drink their healths, and don't be angry.

KITE. Let me see your hand then, once more – Here has been gold – five guineas, my friend, in this very hand this morning.

BUTCHER. Nay, then he is the devil – Pray, doctor, were you born of a woman, or did you come into the world of your own head?

KITE. That's a secret – This gold was offer'd you by a proper hand-some man, call'd Hawk, or Buzzard, or –

BUTCHER. Kite you mean.

KITE. Aye, aye, Kite.

BUTCHER. As errant a rogue as ever carried a halberd – the impudent rascal would have decoy'd me for a soldier.

KITE. A soldier! A man of your substance for a soldier! Your mother has a hundred pound in hard money lying at this minute in the hands of a mercer, not forty yards from this place.

BUTCHER. Oons, and so she has, but very few know so much.

KITE. I know it, and that rogue, what's his name, Kite, knew it! And offer'd you five guineas to list, because he knew your poor mother would give the hundred for your discharge –

BUTCHER. There's a dog now – Flesh, doctor, I'll give you t' other half crown, and tell me that this same Kite will be hang'd.

KITE. He's in as much danger as any man in the county of Salop.

BUTCHER. There's your fee – but you have forgot the Surgeon General all this while.

KITE. You put the stars in a passion. (*Looks on his books.*) But now they're pacify'd again – Let me see – did you never cut off a man's leg?

BUTCHER. No.

KITE. Recollect, pray.

BUTCHER. I say no.

KITE. That's strange, wonderful strange; but nothing is strange to me, such wonderful changes have I seen – the second, or third, aye, the third campaign that you make in Flanders, the leg of a great officer will be shatter'd by a great shot; you will be there accidentally, and with your cleaver chop off the limb at a blow; in short, the operation will be performed with so much dexterity, that with general applause you will be made Surgeon General of the whole army.

BUTCHER. Nay, for the matter of cutting off a limb – I'll do 't – I'll do 't with any surgeon in Europe, but I have no thoughts of making a campaign.

KITE. You have no thoughts! What matter for your thoughts? The stars have decreed it, and you must go.

BUTCHER. The stars decree it! Oons, sir, the justices can't press me.

KITE. Nay, friend, 'tis none of my business, I ha' done – only mind this – you'll know more an hour and a half hence – that's all – farewell.

Going.

BUTCHER. Hold, hold, doctor, Surgeon General! What is the place worth, pray?

KITE. Five hundred pound a year, beside guineas for claps.

BUTCHER Five hundred pound a year! – An hour and half hence you say?

KITE. Prithee friend be quiet, don't be so troublesome – Here's such a work to make a booby butcher accept of five hundred pound a year – But if you must hear it – I tell you in short, you'll be standing in your stall an hour and half hence, and a gentleman will come by with a snuff-box in his hand, and the tip of his handkerchief hanging out of his right pocket – he'll ask you the price of a loin of veal, and at the same time stroke your great dog upon the head and call him Chopper.

BUTCHER Mercy upon us – Chopper is the dog's name.

KITE. Look 'ee there – what I say is true, things that are to come must come to pass – get you home, sell off your stock, don't mind the whining and the snivelling of your mother and your sister, women always hinder preferment; make what money you can, and follow that gentleman – His name begins with a P – mind that – there will be the barber's daughter, too, that you promis'd marriage to, she will be pulling and haling you to pieces.

BUTCHER. What! Know Sally too? He's the devil, and he needs must go that the devil drives – (*Going*) The tip of his handkerchief out of his left pocket?

KITE. No, no, his right pocket; if it be the left, 'tis none of the man.

BUTCHER Well, well, I'll mind him.

Exit.

PLUME (*behind with his pocket-book*). The right pocket, you say?

KITE. I hear the rustling of silks. (*Knocking.*) Fly, sir, 'tis Madam Melinda.

Enter MELINDA *and* LUCY.

KITE. Tycho, chairs for the ladies.

MELINDA. Don't trouble your self, we shan't stay, doctor.

KITE. Your ladyship is to stay much longer than you imagine.

MELINDA. For what?

KITE. For a husband. – (*To* LUCY.) For your part, madam, you won't stay for a husband.

LUCY. Pray, doctor, do you converse with the stars, or with the devil?

KITE. With both; when I have the destinies of men in search, I consult the stars, when the affairs of women come under my hand, I advise with my t' other friend.

MELINDA. And have you rais'd the devil upon my account?

KITE. Yes, madam, and he's now under the table.

LUCY. Oh! Heavens protect us – dear madam, let us be gone.

KITE. If you be afraid of him, why do you come to consult him?

MELINDA. Don't fear, fool. Do you think, sir, that because I'm a woman I'm to be fool'd out of my reason, or frighted out of my senses? – Come, show me this devil.

KITE. He's a little busy at present, but when he has done he shall wait on you.

MELINDA. What is he doing?

KITE. Writing your name in his pocket-book.

MELINDA. Ha, ha, ha, my name! Pray, what have you or he to do with my name?

KITE. Look 'ee, fair lady – the devil is a very modest person, he seeks no body unless they seek him first; he's chained up like a mastiff, and cannot stir unless he be let loose. – You come to me to have your fortune told – do you think, madam, that I can answer you of my own head? No, madam, the affairs of women are so irregular, that nothing less than the devil can give any account of 'em. Now to convince you of your incredulity, I'll show you a trial of my skill. – Here, you Cacodemon del fuego, exert your power, – draw me this lady's name, the word Melinda, in the proper letters and character of her own hand writing. – Do it at three motions – one, two, three – 'tis done – Now, madam, will you please to send your maid to fetch it.

LUCY. I fetch it! The devil fetch me if I do.

MELINDA. My name in my own hand-writing! That would be
   convincing indeed.

KITE. Seeing's believing.

   Goes to the table, lifts up the carpet.

   Here Tre, Tre, poor Tre, give me the bone, sirrah Oh! oh! the
   devil, the devil in good earnest, my hand, my hand, the devil,
   my hand!

   He puts his hand under the table, PLUME *steals to the other side of the
   table and catches him by the hand.* MELINDA *and* LUCY *shriek, and
   run to a corner of the stage.* KITE *discovers* PLUME *and gets away his
   hand.*

   A plague o' your pincers, he has fixed his nails in my very flesh.
   Oh! madam, you put the demon in such a passion with your
   scruples, that it has almost cost me my hand.

MELINDA. It has cost us our lives almost – but have you got the
   name?

KITE. Got it! Aye, madam, I have got it here – I'm sure the blood
   comes – but there's your name upon that square piece of paper
   – behold –

MELINDA. 'Tis wonderful – my very letters to a tittle.

LUCY. 'Tis like your hand, madam, but not so like your hand
   neither, and now I look nearer, 'tis not like your hand at all.

KITE. Here's a chamber-maid now will out-lie the devil.

LUCY. Look 'ee, madam, they shan't impose upon us; people can't
   remember their hands no more than they can their faces – Come,
   madam, let us be certain, write your name upon this paper –
   (Takes out paper and folds it.) then we'll compare the two names.

KITE. Any thing for your satisfaction, madam – here's pen and ink –

   MELINDA *writes, and* LUCY *holds the paper.*

LUCY. Let me see it, madam, 'tis the same, the very same. – *(Aside.)*
   But I'll secure one copy for my own affairs.

MELINDA. This is demonstration.

KITE. 'Tis so, madam, the word demonstration comes from Demon the father of lies.

MELINDA. Well, doctor, I'm convinc'd; and now pray what account can you give me of my future fortune?

KITE. Before the sun has made one course round this earthly globe, your fortune will be fixed for happiness or misery.

MELINDA. What! so near the crisis of my fate!

KITE. Let me see – about the hour of ten to morrow morning you will be saluted by a gentleman who will come to take his leave of you, being design'd for travel. His intention of going abroad is sudden, and the occasion a woman. Your fortune and his are like the bullet and the barrel, one runs plump into the t' other – in short, if the gentleman travels he will die abroad; and if he does you will die before he comes home.

MELINDA. What sort of man is he?

KITE. Madam, he's a fine gentleman, and a lover – that is, a man of very good sense, and a very great fool.

MELINDA. How is that possible, doctor?

KITE. Because, madam, – because it is so: a woman's reason is the best for a man's being a fool.

MELINDA. Ten o'clock, you say?

KITE. Ten, about the hour of tea-drinking throughout the kingdom.

MELINDA. Here, doctor. (*Gives him money.*) Lucy, have you any questions to ask?

LUCY. Oh! Madam, a thousand.

KITE. I must beg your patience till another time, for I expect more company this minute; besides, I must discharge the gentleman under the table.

LUCY. Oh, pray, sir, discharge us first.

KITE. Tycho, wait on the ladies down stairs.

Exit MELINDA *and* LUCY. *Enter* PLUME *and* WORTHY.

KITE. Aye, you may well laugh, gentlemen, not all the cannon of the French army could have frighted me so much as that gripe you gave me under the table.

PLUME. I think, Mr. Doctor, I out-conjur'd you that bout.

KITE. I was surpris'd, for I should not have taken a captain for a conjurer.

PLUME. No more than I should a sergeant for a wit.

KITE. Mr. Worthy, you were pleas'd to wish me joy to day, I hope to be able to return the compliment tomorrow.

WORTHY. I'll make it the best compliment to you that ever I made in my life, if you do; but I must be a traveller you say?

KITE. No farther than the chops of the Channel, I presume, sir.

PLUME. That we have concerted already. (*Knocking hard.*) Hey day! You don't profess midwifry, doctor?

KITE. Away to your ambuscade.

Exeunt PLUME *and* WORTHY. *Enter* BRAZEN.

BRAZEN. Your servant, servant, my dear.

KITE. Stand off – I have my familiar already.

BRAZEN Are you bewitch'd, my dear?

KITE. Yes, my dear, but mine is a peaceable spirit, and hates gunpowder – thus I fortify myself, (*Draws a circle round him.*) and now, Captain, have a care how you force my lines.

BRAZEN. Lines! what dost talk of lines? You have something like a fishing rod there, indeed; but I come to be acquainted with you, man – what's your name, my dear?

KITE. Conundrum.

BRAZEN. Conundrum! Rat me, I know a famous doctor in London of your name, where were you born?

KITE. I was born in Algebra.

BRAZEN. Algebra! – 'Tis no country in Christendom I'm sure, unless it be some pitiful place in the Highlands of Scotland.

KITE. Right! I told you I was bewitch'd.

BRAZEN. So am I, my dear, I'm going to be married. – I've had two letters from a lady of fortune that loves me to madness, fits, colic, spleen, and vapours – shall I marry her in four and twenty hours, aye or no?

KITE. I must have the year and day o' th' month when these letters were dated.

BRAZEN. Why, you old bitch, did you ever hear of love-letters dated with the year and day o' th' month? Do you think billets doux are like bank bills?

KITE. They are not so good – but if they bear no date, I must examine the contents.

BRAZEN. Contents, that you shall, old boy, here they be both.

KITE. Only the last you receiv'd, if you please (*Takes the letter.*) Now, sir, if you please to let me consult my books for a minute, I'll send this letter enclos'd to you with the determination of the stars upon it to your lodgings.

BRAZEN. With all my heart – I must give him – (*Puts his hand in's pocket.*) Algebra! I fancy, doctor, 'tis hard to calculate the place of your nativity – Here – (*Gives him money.*) and if I succeed, I'll build a watch-tower upon the top of the highest mountain in Wales for the study of astrology, and the benefit of Conundrums.

Exit. Enter PLUME *and* WORTHY.

WORTHY. Oh! Doctor, that letter's worth a million, let me see it – and now I have it, I'm afraid to open it.

PLUME. Pho, let me see it! (*Opening the letter.*) If she be a jilt – damn her, she is one – there's her name at the bottom on 't.

WORTHY. How! – then I will travel in good earnest – by all my hopes, 'tis Lucy's hand.

PLUME. Lucy's!

WORTHY. Certainly, 'tis no more like Melinda's character than black is to white.

PLUME. Then 'tis certainly Lucy's contrivance to draw in Brazen for a husband – but are you sure 'tis not Melinda's hand?

WORTHY. You shall see; where's the bit of paper I gave you just now that the devil writ Melinda upon.

KITE. Here, sir.

PLUME. 'Tis plain, they're not the same; and is this the malicious name that was subscrib'd to the letter which made Mr. Balance send his daughter into the country?

WORTHY. The very same, the other fragments I show'd you just now, I once intended it for another use, but I think I have turn'd it now to better advantage.

PLUME. But 'twas barbarous to conceal this so long, and to continue me so many hours in the pernicious heresy of believing that angelic creature could change – poor Silvia!

WORTHY. Rich Silvia, you mean, and poor Captain – ha, ha, ha; come, come, friend, Melinda is true, and shall be mine; Silvia is constant, and may be yours.

PLUME. No, she's above my hopes – but for her sake I'll recant my opinion of her sex.

> *By some the sex is blam'd without design,*
> *Light, harmless censure, such as yours and mine,*
> *Sallies of wit, and vapours of our wine.*
> *Others the justice of the sex condemn,*
> *And wanting merit to create esteem,*
> *would hide their own defects by cens'ring them.*
> *But they, secure in their all-conqu'ring charms*
> *Laugh at the vain efforts of false alarms,*
> *He magnifies their conquests who complains,*
> *For none would struggle were they not in chains.*

Exeunt.

The end of the fourth act.

Act V, Scene i

An antechamber, with a periwig, hat, and sword upon the table.
Enter SILVIA *in her night cap.*

SILVIA. I have rested but indifferently, and I believe my bedfellow
was as little pleas'd; poor Rose! here she comes –

Enter ROSE.

Good morrow, my dear, how d' ye this morning?

ROSE. Just as I was last night, neither better nor worse for you.

SILVIA. What's the matter? did you not like your bedfellow?

ROSE. I don't know whether I had a bedfellow or not.

SILVIA. Did not I lie with you?

ROSE. No – I wonder you could have the conscience to ruin a
poor girl for nothing.

SILVIA. I have sav'd thee from ruin, child; don't be melancholy,
I can give you as many fine things as the Captain can.

ROSE. But you can't I'm sure.

Knocking at the door.

SILVIA. Odso! my accoutrements –

Puts on her periwig, hat and sword.

Who's at the door?

MOB. Open the door, or we'll break it down.

SILVIA. Patience a little –

Opens the door. Enter CONSTABLE *and* MOB.

CONSTABLE. We have 'um, we have 'um, the duck and the mallard both in the decoy.

SILVIA. What means this riot? Stand off – (*Draws.*) The man dies that comes within reach of my point.

CONSTABLE. That is not the point, master, put up your sword or I shall knock you down; and so I command the Queen's peace.

SILVIA. You are some blockhead of a constable.

CONSTABLE. I am so, and have a warrant to apprehend the bodies of you and your whore there.

ROSE. Whore! never was poor woman so abus'd.

Enter BULLOCK *unbutton'd.*

BULLOCK. What's matter now? – Oh! Mr. Bridewell, what brings you abroad so early?

CONSTABLE. This, sir – (*Lays hold of* BULLOCK.) You're the Queen's prisoner.

BULLOCK. Wauns, you lie, sir, I'm the Queen's soldier.

CONSTABLE. No matter for that, you shall go before Justice Balance.

SILVIA. Balance! 'Tis what I wanted – here, Mr. Constable, I resign my sword.

ROSE. Can't you carry us before the Captain, Mr. Bridewell?

CONSTABLE. Captain! ha'n't you got your belly full of captains yet? Come, come, make way there.

Exeunt.

Act V, Scene ii

Scene, Justice Balance's house. BALANCE *and* SCALE.

SCALE. I say 'tis not to be borne, Mr. Balance.

BALANCE. Look 'ee, Mr. Scale, for my own part I shall be very tender in what regards the officers of the army; they expose their lives to so many dangers for us abroad, that we may give them some grains of allowance at home.

SCALE. Allowance! This poor girl's father is my tenant, and if I mistake not, her mother nursed a child for you; shall they debauch our daughters to our faces?

BALANCE. Consider, Mr. Scale, that were it not for the bravery of these officers we should have French dragoons among us, that would leave us neither liberty, property, wife, nor daughter. – Come, Mr. Scale, the gentlemen are vigorous and warm, and may they continue so; the same heat that stirs them up to love, spurs them on to battle: you never knew a great general in your life, that did not love a whore – this I only speak in reference to Captain Plume, – for the other spark I know nothing of.

SCALE. Nor can I hear of anybody that do's – oh! here they come.

Enter SILVIA, BULLOCK, ROSE, PRISONERS; CONSTABLE *and* MOB.

CONSTABLE. May it please your worships, we took them in the very act, *re infecta*, sir; the gentleman indeed behav'd himself like a gentleman, for he drew his sword and swore, and afterwards laid it down and said nothing.

BALANCE. Give the gentleman his sword again – wait you without.

Exeunt CONSTABLE *etc.*

(*To* SILVIA.) I'm sorry, sir, to know a gentleman upon such terms, that the occasion of our meeting should prevent the satisfaction of an acquaintance.

SILVIA. Sir, you need make no apology for your warrant, no more than I shall do for my behaviour. – My innocence is upon an equal foot with your authority.

SCALE. Innocence! have you not seduc'd that young maid?

SILVIA. No, Mr. Goose-cap, she seduc'd me.

BULLOCK. So she did I'll swear, – for she propos'd marriage first.

BALANCE. What! then you're married, child? (*To* ROSE.)

ROSE. Yes, sir, to my sorrow.

BALANCE. Who was witness?

BULLOCK. That was I – I danc'd, threw the stocking, and spoke jokes by their bed-side, I'm sure.

BALANCE. Who was the minister?

BULLOCK. Minister! we are soldiers, and want no ministers – they were married by the Articles of War.

BALANCE. Hold thy prating, fool; your appearance, sir, promises some understanding; pray, what does this fellow mean?

SILVIA. He means marriage, I think, – but that, you know, is so odd a thing, that hardly any two people under the sun agree in the ceremony; some make it a sacrament, others a convenience, and others make it a jest; but among soldiers 'tis most sacred – our sword, you know, is our honour, that we lay down, the hero jumps over it first, and the amazon after – leap rogue, follow whore, the drum beats a ruff, and so to bed; that's all, the ceremony is concise.

BULLOCK. And the prettiest ceremony, so full of pastime and prodigality –

BALANCE. What! are you a soldier?

BULLOCK. Aye, that I am – will your worship lend me your cane, and I'll show you how I can exercise.

BALANCE. Take it. (*Strikes him over the head. To* SILVIA.) Pray, sir, what commission may you bear?

SILVIA. I'm call'd Captain, sir, by all the coffee-men, drawers, whores, and groom porters in London, for I wear a red coat, a sword *bien troussé*, a martial twist in my cravat, a fierce knot in my periwig, a cane upon my button; picket in my head, and dice in my pocket.

SCALE. Your name, pray sir?

SILVIA. Captain Pinch; I cock my hat with a pinch, I take snuff with a pinch, pay my whores with a pinch; in short, I can do any thing at a pinch, but fight and fill my belly.

BALANCE. And pray, sir, what brought you into Shropshire?

SILVIA. A pinch, sir: I knew you country gentlemen want wit, and you know that we town gentlemen want money, and so −

BALANCE. I understand you, sir; − here, Constable −

Enter CONSTABLE.

Take this gentleman into custody till farther orders.

ROSE. Pray your worship, don't be uncivil to him, for he did me no hurt; he's the most harmless man in the world, for all he talks so.

SCALE. Come, come, child, I'll take care of you.

SILVIA. What, gentlemen, rob me of my freedom and my wife at once! 'tis the first time they ever went together.

BALANCE (*whispers the* CONSTABLE). Hark 'ee, Constable −

CONSTABLE. It shall be done, sir, − Come along, sir.

Exeunt CONSTABLE, BULLOCK *and* SILVIA.

BALANCE. Come, Mr. Scale, we'll manage the spark presently.

Exeunt BALANCE *and* SCALE.

Act V, Scene iii

Scene changes to MELINDA's *apartment.* MELINDA *and* WORTHY.

MELINDA (*aside*). So far the prediction is right, 'tis ten exactly; and pray, sir, how long have you been in this travelling humour?

WORTHY. 'Tis natural, madam, for us to avoid what disturbs our quiet.

MELINDA. Rather the love of change, which is more natural, may
be the occasion of it.

WORTHY. To be sure, madam, there must be charms in variety,
else neither you nor I should be so fond of it.

MELINDA. You mistake, Mr. Worthy, I am not so fond of variety, as
to travel for it; nor do I think it prudence in you to run your self
into a certain expense and danger, in hopes of precarious
pleasures, which at best never answer expectation, as 'tis evident
from the example of most travellers, that long more to return to
their own country than they did to go abroad.

WORTHY. What pleasures I may receive abroad are indeed
uncertain; but this I am sure of, I shall meet with less cruelty
among the most barbarous nations, than I have found at home.

MELINDA. Come, sir, you and I have been jangling a great while –
I fancy if we made up our accounts, we should the sooner come
to an agreement.

WORTHY. Sure, madam, you won't dispute your being in my
debt – my fears, sighs, vows, promises, assiduities, anxieties,
jealousies, have run on for a whole year, without any payment.

MELINDA. A year! O Mr. Worthy, what you owe to me is not to be
paid under a seven years servitude; how did you use me the year
before, when taking the advantage of my innocence and
necessity, you would have made me your mistress, that is, your
slave – remember the wicked insinuations, artful baits, deceitful
arguments, cunning pretences; then your impudent behaviour,
loose expressions, familiar letters, rude visits; remember those,
those Mr. Worthy.

WORTHY (aside). I do remember, and am sorry I made no better
use of 'em. But you may remember, madam – that –

MELINDA. Sir, I'll remember nothing, 'tis your interest that I should
forget; you have been barbarous to me, I have been cruel to you
– put that and that together, and let one balance the other – Now
if you will begin upon a new score, lay aside your adventuring
airs, and behave yourself handsomely till Lent be over – here's
my hand, I'll use you as a gentleman should be.

WORTHY. And if I don't use you as a gentlewoman should be, may this be my poison. (*Kissing her hand.*)

Enter SERVANT.

SERVANT. Madam, the coach is at the door.

MELINDA. I'm going to Mr. Balance's country-house to see my cousin Silvia, I have done her an injury, and can't be easy till I have ask'd her pardon.

WORTHY. I dare not hope for the honour of waiting on you.

MELINDA. My coach is full, but if you will be so gallant as to mount your own horses and follow us, we shall be glad to be overtaken; and if you bring Captain Plume with you, we shan't have the worse reception.

WORTHY. I'll endeavour it.

Exit WORTHY, *leading* MELINDA.

Act V, Scene iv

Scene, the market-place. PLUME *and* KITE.

PLUME. A baker, a tailor, a smith, and a butcher – I believe the first colony planted at Virginia had not more trades in their company than I have in mine.

KITE. The butcher, sir, will have his hands full; for we have two sheep-stealers among us – I hear of a fellow too committed just now for stealing of horses.

PLUME. We'll dispose of him among the dragoons – have we never a poulterer among us?

KITE. Yes, sir, the king of the gypsies is a very good one, he has an excellent hand at a goose, or a turkey – Here's Captain Brazen – sir, I must go look after the men.

Exit. Enter BRAZEN *reading a letter.*

BRAZEN. Um, um, um, the canonical hour – um, um, very well. –
My dear Plume! Give me a buss.

PLUME. Half a score if you will, my dear; what hast got in thy
hand, child?

BRAZEN 'Tis a project for laying out a thousand pound.

PLUME. Were it not requisite to project first how to get it in?

BRAZEN. You can't imagine, my dear, that I want twenty thousand
pound; I have spent twenty times as much in the service – Now,
my dear, pray advise me; my head runs much upon architecture;
shall I build a privateer or a play-house?

PLUME. An odd question – a privateer or a playhouse! 'Twill
require some consideration – faith, I'm for a privateer.

BRAZEN. I'm not of your opinion, my dear – for in the first place
a privateer may be ill built.

PLUME. And so may a play-house.

BRAZEN. But a privateer may be ill-mann'd.

PLUME. And so may a play-house.

BRAZEN. But a privateer may run upon the shallows.

PLUME. Not so often as a play-house.

BRAZEN. But, you know, a privateer may spring a leak.

PLUME. And I know that a play-house may spring a great many.

BRAZEN. But suppose the privateer come home with a rich booty,
we should never agree about our shares.

PLUME. 'Tis just so in a play-house – so by my advice, you shall
fix upon the privateer.

BRAZEN. Agreed – but if this twenty thousand should not be *in
specie* –

PLUME. What twenty thousand?

BRAZEN. Hark 'ee – (*Whispers.*)

PLUME. Married!

BRAZEN. Presently, we're to meet about half a mile out of town at the water-side – And so forth – (*Reads.*) 'For fear I should be known by any of Worthy's friends, you must give me leave to wear my mask till after the ceremony, which will make me ever yours.' – Look 'ee there, my dear dog.

Shows the bottom of the letter to PLUME.

PLUME. Melinda! And by this light, her own hand! – Once more, if you please, my dear; her hand exactly! – Just now you say?

BRAZEN. This minute I must be gone.

PLUME. Have a little patience, and I'll go with you.

BRAZEN. No, no, I see a gentleman coming this way that may be inquisitive; 'tis Worthy, do you know him?

PLUME. By sight only.

BRAZEN. Have a care, the very eyes discover secrets –

Exit. Enter WORTHY.

WORTHY. To boot and saddle, Captain, you must mount.

PLUME. Whip and spur, Worthy, or you won't mount.

WORTHY. But I shall: Melinda and I are agreed, she is gone to visit Silvia; we are to mount and follow, and could we carry a parson with us, who knows what might be done for us both?

PLUME. Don't trouble your head, Melinda has secured a parson already.

WORTHY. Already! Do you know more than I?

PLUME. Yes, I saw it under her hand – Brazen and she are to meet half a mile hence at the water-side, there to take boat, I suppose to be ferried over to the Elysian fields, if there be any such thing in matrimony.

WORTHY. I parted with Melinda just now; she assur'd me she hated Brazen, and that she resolv'd to discard Lucy for daring to write letters to him in her name.

PLUME. Nay, nay, there's nothing of Lucy in this – I tell ye I saw Melinda's hand as surely as this is mine.

WORTHY. But I tell you, she's gone this minute to Justice Balance's country house.

PLUME. But I tell you, she's gone this minute to the water-side.

Enter a SERVANT.

SERVANT (*to* WORTHY). Sir, Madam Melinda has sent word that you need not trouble your self to follow her; because her journey to Justice Balance's is put off, and she's gone to take the air another way.

WORTHY. How! Her journey put off?

PLUME. That is, her journey was a put-off to you.

WORTHY. 'Tis plain, plain – but how, where, when is she to meet Brazen?

PLUME. Just now, I tell you, half a mile hence at the water-side.

WORTHY. Up, or down the water?

PLUME. That I don't know.

WORTHY. I'm glad my horses are ready – Jack, get 'em out.

PLUME. Shall I go with you?

WORTHY. Not an inch – I shall return presently.

Exit.

PLUME. You'll find me at the hall; the justices are sitting by this time, and I must attend them.

Exit.

Act V, Scene v

Scene, a court of justice. BALANCE, SCALE, SCRUPLE *upon the bench.* CONSTABLE, MOB, KITE. KITE *and* CONSTABLE *advance to the front of the stage.*

KITE. Pray, who are those honourable gentlemen upon the bench?

CONSTABLE. He in the middle is Justice Balance, he on the right is Justice Scale, and he on the left is Justice Scruple, and I am Mr. Constable, four very honest gentlemen.

KITE. O dear sir, I'm your most obedient servant. (*Saluting the* CONSTABLE.) I fancy, sir, that your employment and mine are much the same, for my business is to keep people in order, and if they disobey, to knock 'em down; and then we're both staff-officers.

CONSTABLE. Nay, I'm a sergeant myself – of the militia – Come, brother, you shall see me exercise – Suppose this a musket now, (*He puts his staff on his right shoulder.*) now I'm shoulder'd.

KITE. Aye, you're shoulder'd pretty well for a constable's staff, but for a musket you must put it on t' other shoulder, my dear.

CONSTABLE. Adso, that's true, – come, now give the word o' command.

KITE. Silence.

CONSTABLE. Aye, aye, so we will, – we will be silent.

KITE. Silence, you dog, silence –

Strikes him over the head with his halberd.

CONSTABLE. That's the way to silence a man with a witness – What d' ye mean, friend?

KITE. Only to exercise you, sir.

CONSTABLE. Your exercise differs so from ours, that we shall ne'er agree about it; if my own captain had given me such a rap I had taken the law of him.

Enter PLUME.

BALANCE. Captain, you're welcome.

PLUME. Gentlemen, I thank'ee.

SCRUPLE. Come, honest Captain, sit by me.

PLUME *ascends, and sits upon the bench.*

Now produce your prisoners – Here, that fellow there, – set him up – Mr. Constable, what have you to say against this man?

CONSTABLE. I have nothing to say against him, an't please ye.

BALANCE. No? What made you bring him hither?

CONSTABLE. I don't know, an't please your worship.

SCRUPLE. Did not the contents of your warrant direct you what sort of men to take up?

CONSTABLE. I can't tell, an't please ye, I can't read.

SCRUPLE. A very pretty constable truly! I find we have no business here.

KITE. May it please the worshipful bench, I desire to be heard in this case, as being counsel for the Queen.

BALANCE. Come, Sergeant, you shall be heard, since nobody else will speak; we won't come here for nothing –

KITE. This man is but one man, the country may spare him and the army wants him, besides, he's cut out by nature for a grenadier, he's five foot ten inches high, he shall box, wrestle, or dance the Cheshire Round with any man in the county, he gets drunk every sabbath-day, and he beats his wife.

WIFE. You lie, sirrah, you lie, an't please your worship, he's the best natur'd, pains-taking man in the parish, witness my five poor children.

SCRUPLE. A wife and five children! you Constable, you rogue, how durst you impress a man that has a wife and five children?

SCALE. Discharge him, discharge him.

BALANCE. Hold, gentlemen – hark 'ee, friend, how do you maintain your wife and five children?

PLUME. They live upon wild fowl and venison, sir, the husband keeps a gun, and kills all the hares and partridges within five miles round.

BALANCE. A gun! Nay, if he be so good at gunning he shall have enough on 't – He may be of use against the French, for he shoots flying to be sure.

SCRUPLE. But his wife and children, Mr. Balance!

WIFE. Aye, aye, that's the reason you would send him away – You know I have a child every year, and you're afraid they should come upon the parish at last.

PLUME. Look 'ee there, gentlemen, the honest woman has spoke it at once; the parish had better maintain five children this year than six or seven the next; that fellow upon his high feeding may get you two or three beggars at a birth.

WIFE. Look 'ee, Mr. Captain, the parish shall get nothing by sending him away, for I won't lose my teeming time if there be a man left in the parish.

BALANCE. Send that woman to the house of correction – and the man –

KITE. I'll take care o' him, if you please.

Takes the MAN down.

SCALE. Here, you constable, the next – set up that black-fac'd fellow, he has a gunpowder look, what can you say against this man, constable?

CONSTABLE. Nothing, but that he's a very honest man.

PLUME. Pray, gentlemen, let me have one honest man in my company for the novelty's sake.

BALANCE. What are you, friend?

SECOND PRISONER. A collier, I work in the coalpits.

SCRUPLE. Look 'ee, gentlemen, this fellow has a trade, and the Act of Parliament here expresses, that we are to impress no man that has any visible means of a livelihood.

KITE. May it please your worships, this man has no visible means of a livelihood, for he works under-ground.

PLUME. Well said, Kite – besides, the army wants miners.

BALANCE. Right! and had we an order of government for 't, we could raise you in this and the neighbouring county of Stafford five hundred colliers that would run you under-ground like moles, and do more service in a siege that all the miners in the army.

SCRUPLE. Well, friend, what have you to say for your self?

SECOND PRISONER. I'm married.

KITE. Lack-a-day, so am I.

SECOND PRISONER. Here's my wife, poor woman.

BALANCE. Are you married, good woman?

WOMAN. I'm married in conscience.

KITE. May it please your worship, she's with child in conscience.

SCALE. Who married you, mistress?

WOMAN. My husband – we agreed that I should call him husband to avoid passing for a whore, and that he should call me wife to shun going for a soldier.

SCRUPLE. A very pretty couple – pray, Captain, will you take 'em both?

PLUME. What say you, Mr. Kite – will you take care of the woman?

KITE. Yes, sir, she shall go with us to the sea-side and there if she has a mind to drown her self, we'll take care that no body shall hinder her.

BALANCE. Here, Constable, bring in my man.

Exit CONSTABLE.

Now, Captain, I'll fit you with a man such as you ne'er listed in your life.

Enter CONSTABLE *and* SILVIA.

Oh my friend Pinch – I'm very glad to see you.

SILVIA. Well sir, and what then?

SCALE. What then! Is that your respect to the bench?

SILVIA. Sir, I don't care a farthing for you nor your bench neither.

SCRUPLE. Look 'ee, gentlemen, that's enough, he's a very impudent fellow, and fit for a soldier.

SCALE. A notorious rogue, I say, and very fit for a soldier.

CONSTABLE. A whoremaster, I say, and therefore fit to go.

BALANCE. What think you, Captain?

PLUME. I think he's a very pretty fellow, and therefore fit to serve.

SILVIA. Me for a soldier! Send your own lazy, lubberly sons at home, fellows that hazard their necks every day in pursuit of a fox, yet dare not peep abroad to look an enemy in the face.

CONSTABLE. May it please your worships, I have a woman at the door to swear a rape against this rogue.

SILVIA. Is it your wife or daughter, booby? I ravished 'em both yesterday.

BALANCE. Pray, Captain, read the Articles of War, we'll see him listed immediately.

PLUME (*reads*). 'Articles of War against Mutiny and Desertion.'

SILVIA. Hold, sir – Once more, gentlemen, have a care what you do, for you shall severely smart for any violence you offer to me, and you, Mr. Balance, I speak to you particularly, you shall heartily repent it.

PLUME. Look 'ee, young spark, say but one word more and I'll build a horse for you as high as the ceiling, and make you ride the most tiresome journey that ever you made in your life.

SILVIA. You have made a fine speech, good Captain Huffcap – but you had better be quiet, I shall find a way to cool your courage.

PLUME. Pray, gentlemen, don't mind him, he's distracted.

SILVIA. 'Tis false – I'm descended of as good a family as any in your county, my father is as good a man as any upon your bench, and I am heir to twelve hundred pound a year.

BALANCE. He's certainly mad, – pray, Captain, read the Articles of War.

SILVIA. Hold, once more, – pray, Mr. Balance, to you I speak, suppose I were your child, would you use me at this rate?

BALANCE. No faith, were you mine, I would send you to Bedlam first, and into the army afterwards.

SILVIA. But consider, my father, sir, he's as good, as generous, as brave, as just a man as ever serv'd his country; I'm his only child, perhaps the loss of me may break his heart.

BALANCE. He's a very great fool if it does. Captain, if you don't list him this minute, I'll leave the court.

PLUME. Kite, do you distribute the levy money to the men whilst I read.

KITE. Aye, sir, – silence gentlemen.

PLUME *reads the Articles of War.*

BALANCE. Very well; now, Captain, let me beg the favour of you not to discharge this fellow upon any account whatsoever. – Bring in the rest.

CONSTABLE. There are no more, an't please your worship.

BALANCE. No more! there were five two hours ago.

SILVIA. 'Tis true, sir, but this rogue of a constable let the rest escape for a bribe of eleven shillings a man, because he said that the Act allows him but ten, so the odd shilling was clear gains.

ALL JUSTICES. How!

SILVIA. Gentlemen, he offer'd to let me get away for two guineas, but I had not so much about me. – This is truth, and I'm ready to swear it.

KITE. And I'll swear it, give me the book, 'tis for the good of the service.

SECOND PRISONER. May it please your worship, I gave him half a crown to say that I was an honest man, – and now that your worships have made me a rogue, I hope I shall have my money again.

BALANCE. 'Tis my opinion that this constable be put into the Captain's hands, and if his friends don't bring four good men for his ransom by tomorrow night, – Captain, you shall carry him to Flanders.

SCALE, SCRUPLE. Agreed, agreed!

PLUME. Mr. Kite, take the constable into custody.

KITE. Aye, aye, sir, – (*To the* CONSTABLE.) will you please to have your office taken from you, or will you handsomely lay down your staff as your betters have done before you?

The CONSTABLE *drops his staff.*

BALANCE. Come, gentlemen, there needs no great ceremony in adjourning this court; – Captain you shall dine with me.

KITE. Come Mr. Militia Sergeant, I shall silence you now I believe, without your taking the law of me.

Exeunt omnes.

Act V, Scene vi

Scene changes to the fields, BRAZEN *leading in* LUCY *mask'd.*

BRAZEN. The boat is just below here.

Enter WORTHY *with a case of pistols under his arm, parts* BRAZEN *and* LUCY.

WORTHY. Here, sir, take your choice.

Offering the pistols.

BRAZEN. What! Pistols! Are they charg'd, my dear?

WORTHY. With a brace of bullets each.

BRAZEN. But I'm a foot officer, my dear, and never use pistols, the sword is my way, and I won't be put out of my road to please any man.

WORTHY. Nor I neither, so have at you. (*Cocks one pistol.*)

BRAZEN. Look 'ee, my dear, I don't care for pistols; – pray oblige me and let us have a bout at sharps; damn't there's no parrying these bullets.

WORTHY. Sir, if you han't your belly full of these, the swords shall come in for second course.

BRAZEN. Why then fire and fury! I have eaten smoke from the mouth of a cannon; sir, don't think I fear powder, for I live upon 't; let me see, (*Takes a pistol.*) and now, sir, how many paces distant shall we fire?

WORTHY. Fire when you please, I'll reserve my shot till I be sure of you.

BRAZEN. Come, where's your cloak?

WORTHY. Cloak! what d' ye mean?

BRAZEN. To fight upon, I always fight upon a cloak, 'tis our way abroad.

LUCY. Come, gentlemen, I'll end the strife.

Pulls off her mask.

WORTHY. Lucy! take her.

BRAZEN. The devil take me if I do – Huzza! (*Fires his pistol.*) D' ye hear, d' ye hear, you plaguey harridan, how those bullets whistle, suppose they had been lodg'd in my gizzard now? –

LUCY. Pray, sir, pardon me.

BRAZEN. I can't tell, child, till I know whether my money be safe; (*Searching his pockets.*) Yes, yes, I do pardon you, – but if I had you in the Rose Tavern, Covent Garden, with three or four hearty rakes, and three or four smart napkins, I would tell you another story, my dear.

Exit.

WORTHY. And was Melinda privy to this?

LUCY. No, sir, she wrote her name upon a piece of paper at the fortune-teller's last night, which I put in my pocket, and so writ above it to the Captain.

WORTHY. And how came Melinda's journey put off?

LUCY. At the town's end she met Mr. Balance's steward, who told her that Mrs. Silvia was gone from her father's, and no body could tell whither.

WORTHY. Silvia gone from her father's! this will be news to Plume. Go home, and tell your lady how near I was being shot for her.

Exeunt.

Act V, Scene vii

[*Scene,* BALANCE's *house.*] *Enter* BALANCE *with a napkin in his hand, as risen from dinner, talking with his* STEWARD.

STEWARD. We did not miss her till the evening, sir, and then searching for her in the chamber that was my young master's, we found her clothes there, but the suit that your son left in the press when he went to London, was gone.

BALANCE. The white, trimm'd with silver!

STEWARD. The same.

BALANCE. You han't told that circumstance to any body?

STEWARD. To none but your worship.

BALANCE. And be sure you don't. Go into the dining-room, and tell Captain Plume that I beg to speak with him.

STEWARD. I shall.

Exit.

BALANCE. Was ever man so impos'd upon? I had her promise indeed that she should never dispose of herself without my consent. – I have consented with a witness, given her away as my act and deed; and this, I warrant, the Captain thinks will pass; no, I shall never pardon him the villainy, first of robbing me of my daughter, and then the mean opinion he must have of me to think that I could be so wretchedly imposed upon; her extravagant passion might encourage her in the attempt, but the contrivance must be his – I'll know the truth presently.

Enter PLUME.

Pray, Captain, what have you done with your young gentleman soldier?

PLUME. He's at my quarters, I suppose, with the rest of my men.

BALANCE. Does he keep company with the common soldiers?

PLUME. No, he's generally with me.

BALANCE. He lies with you, I presume?

PLUME. No, faith, – I offer'd him part of my bed, but the young rogue fell in love with Rose, and has lain with her, I think since he came to town.

BALANCE. So that between you both, Rose has been finely manag'd.

PLUME. Upon my honour, sir, she had no harm from me.

BALANCE. All's safe, I find – Now, Captain, you must know that the young fellow's impudence in court was well grounded; he said I should heartily repent his being listed, and so I do from my soul.

PLUME. Aye! for what reason?

BALANCE. Because he is no less than what he said he was, born of as good a family as any in this county, and is heir to twelve hundred pound a year.

PLUME. I'm very glad to hear it, for I wanted but a man of that quality to make my company a perfect representative of the whole commons of England.

BALANCE. Won't you discharge him?

PLUME. Not under a hundred pound sterling.

BALANCE. You shall have it, for his father is my intimate friend.

PLUME. Then you shall have him for nothing.

BALANCE. Nay, sir, you shall have your price.

PLUME. Not a penny, sir; I value an obligation to you much above a hundred pound.

BALANCE. Perhaps, sir, you shan't repent your generosity. – Will you please to write his discharge in my pocket book? (*Gives his book.*) In the mean time we'll send for the gentleman. Who waits there?

Enter SERVANT

Go to the Captain's lodgings, and inquire for Mr. Wilful, tell him his captain wants him here immediately.

SERVANT. Sir, the gentleman's below at the door inquiring for the Captain.

PLUME. Bid him come up – here's the discharge, sir.

BALANCE. Sir, I thank you – (*Aside.*) 'Tis plain he had no hand in 't.

Enter SILVIA.

SILVIA. I think, Captain, you might have used me better, than to leave me yonder among your swearing, drunken crew, and you, Mr. Justice, might have been so civil as to have invited me to dinner, for I have eaten with as good a man as your worship.

PLUME. Sir, you must charge our want of respect upon our ignorance of your quality – but now you're at liberty – I have discharg'd you.

SILVIA. Discharg'd me!

BALANCE. Yes, sir, and you must once more go home to your father.

SILVIA. My father! then I'm discovered – Oh, sir, (*Kneeling.*) I expect no pardon.

BALANCE. Pardon! no, no, child; your crime shall be your punishment; here, Captain, I deliver her over to the conjugal power for her chastisement; since she will be a wife, be you a husband, a very husband: when she tells you of her love, upbraid her with her folly; be modishly ungrateful, because she has been unfashionably kind; and use her worse than you would any body else, because you can't use her so well as she deserves.

PLUME. And are you Silvia in good earnest?

SILVIA. Earnest! I have gone too far to make it a jest, sir.

PLUME. And do you give her to me in good earnest?

BALANCE. If you please to take her, sir.

PLUME. Why then I have sav'd my legs and arms, and lost my liberty; secure from wounds, I'm prepar'd for the gout, farewell subsistence, and welcome taxes – Sir, my liberty and hopes of being a general are much dearer to me than your twelve hundred pound a year, but to your love, madam, I resign my freedom, and to your beauty, my ambition; greater in obeying at your feet, than commanding at the head of an army.

Enter WORTHY.

WORTHY. I'm sorry to hear, Mr. Balance, that your daughter is lost.

BALANCE. So am not I, sir, since an honest gentleman has found her.

Enter MELINDA.

MELINDA. Pray, Mr. Balance, what's become of my cousin Silvia?

BALANCE. Your cousin Silvia is talking yonder with your cousin Plume.

MELINDA *and* WORTHY. How!

SILVIA. Do you think it strange, cousin, that a woman should change? But, I hope, you'll excuse a change that has proceeded from constancy; I alter'd my outside because I was the same within, and only laid by the woman to make sure of my man; that's my history.

MELINDA. Your history is a little romantic, cousin, but since success has crown'd your adventures you will have the world o' your side, and I shall be willing to go with the tide, provided you pardon an injury I offer'd you in the letter to your father.

PLUME. That injury, madam, was done to me, and the reparation I expect shall be made to my friend; make Mr. Worthy happy, and I shall be satisfied.

MELINDA. A good example, sir, will go a great way – when my cousin is pleas'd to surrender, 'tis probable, I shan't hold out much longer.

Enter BRAZEN.

BRAZEN. Gentlemen, I am yours, madam, I am not yours.

MELINDA. I'm glad on 't, sir.

BRAZEN. So am I – you have got a pretty house here, Mr. Laconic.

BALANCE. 'Tis time to right all mistakes – my name, sir, is Balance.

BRAZEN. Balance! Sir, I'm your most obedient. – I know your whole generation, – had not you an uncle that was governor of the Leeward Islands some years ago?

BALANCE. Did you know him?

BRAZEN. Intimately, sir – he play'd at billiards to a miracle; you had a brother too, that was captain of a fireship – poor Dick, he had the most engaging way with him – of making punch – and then his cabin was so neat – but his boy Jack was the most comical bastard, ha, ha, ha, a pickled dog, I shall never forget him.

PLUME. Well, Captain, are you fix'd in your project yet, are you still for the privateer?

BRAZEN. No, no, I had enough of a privateer just now, I had like to have been pick'd up by a cruiser under false colours, and a French picaroon for aught I know.

PLUME. But have you got your recruits, my dear?

BRAZEN Not a stick, my dear.

PLUME. Probably I shall furnish you.

Enter ROSE *and* BULLOCK.

ROSE. Captain, Captain, I have got loose once more, and have persuaded my sweetheart Cartwheel, to go with us, but you must promise not to part with me again.

SILVIA. I find Mrs. Rose has not been pleas'd with her bedfellow.

ROSE. Bedfellow! I don't know whether I had a bedfellow or not.

SILVIA. Don't be in a passion, child, I was as little pleas'd with your company as you could be with mine.

BULLOCK. Pray, sir, dunna be offended at my sister, she's something underbred – but if you please I'll lie with you in her stead.

PLUME. I have promised, madam, to provide for this girl; now will you be pleas'd to let her wait upon you, or shall I take care of her?

SILVIA. She shall be my charge, sir, you may find it business enough to take care of me.

BULLOCK. Aye, and of me, Captain, for wauns! if ever you lift your hand against me, I'll desert.

PLUME. Captain Brazen shall take care o' that – My dear, instead of the twenty thousand pound you talk'd of, you shall have the twenty brave recruits that I have rais'd, at the rate they cost me – My commission I lay down to be taken up by some braver fellow, that has more merit and less good fortune, whilst I endeavour by the example of this worthy gentleman to serve my Queen and country at home.

With some regret I quit the active field,
Where glory full reward for life does yield;
But the recruiting trade, with all its train,
Of lasting plague, fatigue, and endless pain,
I gladly quit, with my fair spouse to stay,
And raise recruits the matrimonial way.

Finis.

Epilogue

All ladies and gentlemen that are willing to see the comedy call'd
The Recruiting Officer, let them repair to morrow night by six o'clock
to the sign of the Theatre Royal in Drury Lane, and they shall be
kindly entertain'd –

> *We scorn the vulgar ways to bid you come,*
> *Whole Europe now obeys the call of drum.*
> *The soldier, not the poet, here appears,*
> *And beats up for a corps of volunteers:*
> *He finds that music chiefly does delight ye,*
> *And therefore chooses music to invite ye.*

Beat the *Grenadier March* – row, row, tow – Gentlemen, this piece of
music, called an *Overture to a Battle*, was compos'd by a famous Italian
master, and was perform'd with wonderful success, at the great
operas of Vigo, Schellenberg, and Blenheim; it came off with the
applause of all Europe, excepting France; the French found it a little
too rough for their delicatesse.

> *Some that have acted on those glorious stages,*
> *Are here to witness to succeeding ages,*
> *That no music like the Grenadier's engages.*

Ladies, we must own that this music of ours is not altogether so soft
as Bononcini's, yet we dare affirm, that it has laid more people asleep
than all the Camillas in the world; and you'll condescend to own, that
it keeps one awake, better than any opera that ever was acted.

The Grenadier March seems to be a composure excellently adapted to
the genius of the English; for no music was ever follow'd so far by
us, nor with so much alacrity; and with all deference to the present
subscription, we must say that the *Grenadier March* has been subscrib'd
for by the whole Grand Alliance; and we presume to inform the

ladies, that it always has the pre-eminence abroad, and is constantly heard by the tallest, handsomest men in the whole army. In short, to gratify the present taste, our author is now adapting some words to the *Grenadier March*, which he intends to have perform'd to morrow, if the lady who is to sing it should not happen to be sick.

> *This he concludes to be the surest way*
> *To draw you hither, for you'll all obey*
> *Soft music's call, tho' you should damn his play.*

Glossary

beat up – here, 'go recruiting for', as in 'beating' undergrowth to arouse birds or game

Bed of Honour – that is, a soldier's grave

bien troussé – 'well turned out'

bluff – swaggering, boastful

bodkin – hatpin, or any piercing instrument

brevet – promotion to higher rank without increase in pay

broad pieces – large guinea pieces, minted in the reign of Charles II (hence 'Carolus', the Latin form on the coin)

Castle – that is, Shrewsbury Castle

Cheshire round – energetic country dance

chevaux de frise – defensive barricade of *palisadoes* (qv) tipped with iron

chicken and sparagus, song of – 'The Jovial Companions', a popular bawdy ballad

chops of the channel – the western entrance to the English Channel

chopping – healthy, strapping

cornishes – cornices, ornamental mouldings to ceilings

effa ut flat – musical key (F minor) popular for passionate airs

furbelow scarf – fashionably trimmed shawl

Furns . . . Charleroy – invented signs of the Zodiac, based on Kite's travels in Flanders

grass plats – landscaped lawns

guineas for claps – the surgeon's fees for treating cases of gonorrhea

habeas corpus – legal writ to secure property or person

haling – hauling at, tugging

hank – restraint

hart's horn – smelling salts, prepared from antlers

Hochstet – village close to Blenheim, alternative name for the battle

Landen – major battle of the War of the League of Augsburg, 1693

last war – the inconclusive War of the League of Augsburg, 1689-97

lodestones – figuratively, controlling forces

mangeree – Rose means 'orangery', an orange-scented snuff

March beer – strong beer brewed in Spring

Mareschal of France – The Duc de Tallard, taken prisoner at Blenheim

Mechlin – lace from Flanders, a prohibited import

nab – hat, cap

neat's tongue – ox tongue

pad – plodding horse (boringly secure)

palisado – long pointed stake, effective against cavalry

picaroon – small pirate ship

picket – the card game picquet, here pronounced in English

pinners – lace-bordered bonnets

pipe of choice Barcelona – large cask of wine, perhaps booty from the recent capture of that city

pistols – coins worth over half a guinea

Pressing Act – The Act for Raising Recruits, 1704 (see Introduction, p. xiii)

Prettyman – mock-hero of the Duke of Buckingham's burlesque tragedy, *The Rehearsal* (1672)

punk – prostitute

puris naturalibus – state of nature

ravelin – projecting outer defence or fortification

re infecta – 'with business incomplete', though the Constable probably intended 'flagrante delicto', red-handed

rubs – difficulties, obstacles

ruff – a low continuous beating of drums

Savoy – medieval palace in the Strand, converted for use as a barracks

sharps – rapiers without blunted ends

shoot flying – hit a bird in flight

specie, in – in cash, ready money

stracke – measure of grain, around a bushel

Tangerine – pirate ship from Tangiers

terra firma – colloquialism for landed property

tide-waiter – customs official, awaiting ships coming in with the tide

tit – slang for pretty girl

traverse – passage of arms

tricker, drawing of a – pulling a trigger

vapours – melancholy

veni, vidi, vici – 'I came, I saw, I conquered'

Vulcan – the lame husband of the goddess Venus

Ware, great bed of – vast four-poster bed , said to sleep twelve

wauns – dialect form of oath, 'wounds' ('by Christ's wounds')